THE ALLITT INQUIRY

Independent inquiry
relating to
deaths and injuries
on the children's ward at
Grantham and Kesteven
General Hospital
during the period
February to April
1991

London: HMSO

To the Right Honourable Mrs Virginia Bottomley, MP, Her Majesty's Secretary of State for Health, Whitehall SW1

We have the honour to present herewith the Report of our Inquiry relating to deaths and injuries on the Children's Ward at Grantham and Kesteven General Hospital during the period February to April 1991

C. M. Clothier

Sir Cecil Clothier, KCB, QC (Chairman)

Anne MacDonald

Miss C Anne MacDonald, RGN, RSCN, DipN (London) (Member)

David Shaw

Professor David A Shaw, CBE, FRCP, FRCP (Edin) (Member)

<u>REPORT OF THE INDEPENDENT INQUIRY RELATING TO DEATHS AND
INJURIES ON THE CHILDREN'S WARD AT GRANTHAM AND KESTEVEN
GENERAL HOSPITAL DURING THE PERIOD FEBRUARY TO APRIL 1991</u>

CONTENTS   PAGE

APPENDICES

ACKNOWLEDGEMENTS

We acknowledge with the warmest gratitude our indebtedness to our Secretariat, Ms Joanne Jackson and Ms Stephanie Panting. With unfailing efficiency they organised every aspect of our work; and then with equally unflagging patience produced a succession of drafts of our report, as we struggled to get down with precision our findings and conclusions.

We wish also to record our gratitude to Messrs Davies Arnold Cooper, in whose offices we worked, for their generous help with our administrative needs.

CHAPTER ONE: INTRODUCTION AND TERMS OF REFERENCE

1.1   During the months of February to April 1991, there was a series of unexpected events on the children's ward, Ward Four, at Grantham and Kesteven General Hospital (GKGH). Three children died suddenly on the ward, and a baby died at home not long after discharge.   Nine   other   babies   and   children   collapsed unexpectedly, some more than once. All but one of them had to be transferred urgently to the specialist children's units in Nottingham.

1.2   In many of the cases, it seemed to the doctors on Ward Four and in Nottingham that what had happened was unusual, but could be explained on the basis of each child's medical history. Nevertheless,   as   time   went   by   and   more   children   collapsed unexpectedly, medical and nursing staff in Grantham, bewildered by these events, grew deeply alarmed.

1.3   Post mortem examinations were carried out on the children who died and tests to try to determine the cause of their collapse were carried out on each of the children who survived. Most of these tests proved negative. On 12th April, a blood test result showed that one of the children, whose blood sugar had fallen dramatically and inexplicably on three occasions, had been wrongly injected with insulin. During the weeks that followed, the   possibility   that   this   had   happened   accidentally   was eliminated and, as more emergencies occurred on the ward, the suspicion   grew   that   someone   was   deliberately   harming   the children. On 30th April 1991, the police were called to Ward Four to investigate.

1.4   The police investigation took several months.   Gradually more children were added to the list of those who the police suspected had been victims of criminal activity. As events were pieced together a picture emerged of one person, Enrolled Nurse Beverly Allitt, as the likely culprit. She was first arrested and questioned on 21st May 1991, but it was not until November that the police had gathered enough evidence from the complex history of those months on Ward Four to charge her.

1.5 Arising from the events on Ward Four, Beverly Allitt was charged with four murders, nine attempted murders and nine counts of causing grievous bodily harm with intent to the same children. She was also charged with attempting to murder two adults elsewhere and with causing them grievous bodily harm with intent. On days between 13th and 17th May 1993, she was convicted of murdering Liam Taylor, Timothy Hardwick, Becky Phillips and Claire Peck. She was also convicted of attempting to murder Paul Crampton, Bradley Gibson and Katie Phillips, and of causing grievous bodily harm to Kayley Desmond, Yik Hung Chan, Michael Davidson, Christopher Peasgood, Christopher King and Patrick Elstone. She was sentenced to life imprisonment on every count. She was found not guilty of the charges relating to the two adults.

1.6 Once Allitt had been convicted of these crimes, there was an urgent need for an Inquiry into how she had been able to commit them on a children's ward in a National Health Service hospital. The Inquiry which Trent Regional Health Authority had already conducted had been restrained by the impending trial from looking into the tragic events of February to April 1991, and had focused mainly on the existing quality of services for children at GKGH. Now that the trial was over, a wide-ranging independent Inquiry was called for.

1.7 On the instructions of the Secretary of State for Health we were asked in May 1993 to conduct this Inquiry on behalf of Trent Regional Health Authority. Our terms of reference were as follows:

> 1.1 To enquire into the circumstances leading to the deaths of four children and injuries to nine others on Ward 4 at GKGH during the months of February to April 1991 (inclusive);

1.2 To consider the speed and appropriateness of the clinical and managerial response within the hospital to the incidents and to make recommendations;

1.3 To examine the appointment procedures and systems of assessment and supervision within the Hospital and Mid Trent College of Nursing and Midwifery respectively, including an examination of the occupational health services available to both the College and the Hospital and to make recommendations;

1.4 To review the recommendations of the Regional Fact Finding Inquiry into Paediatric Services at the hospital (July 1992) and to advise whether any additions or amendments to those recommendations are necessary;

1.5 In the light of the occurrences on Ward 4 at GKGH between February and April 1991 (inclusive):-

   1.5.1   to advise on the most efficient way for Health Authorities to be informed of serious untoward incidents and to monitor their handling;

   1.5.2   to consider whether and, if so, how the Regional Health Authority should be informed of serious untoward incidents and the way in which they are handled;

1.6 To consider such other matters relating to the said matters as the public interest may require.

1.8 We know that the tragic events on Ward Four were brought about by the hand of Beverly Allitt. In order to inquire into those events, we decided that we should first address ourselves to her as an individual, considering her personality, health, training and finally her entry to the nursing profession. Then we would look also at the surrounding circumstances in which she committed her crimes, including the roles played by other persons, not merely at GKGH but right up to the Regional Health Authority, and the relevant policies and procedures.

1.9 In the course of our Inquiry, we have interviewed a wide range of people. We would like to thank all those we interviewed for their time and the frankness with which most of them spoke of what must have been very painful memories.

1.10 Every inquiry such as this must beware of the wisdom of hindsight. It is impossible to rid the mind of knowledge acquired after the event, which shapes the understanding and may warp the judgment. We have done our best in forming our conclusions not to let them be unduly influenced by facts many of which are now clear, but which must have been mere shadows in a fog of bewilderment to those grappling with events at the time. Nor have we paid much heed to the flow of critical reminiscence which invariably follows the unexpected discovery of someone's misdeeds.

1.11 This report presents our findings and makes recommendations aimed at reducing the chances of such a tragedy as this happening again. Chapter Two examines chronologically Allitt's pathway into nursing and her appointment to Ward Four. Chapter Three takes a similar chronological look at the circumstances of the incidents themselves. Chapter Four looks back and reviews the fragments of evidence which emerged as to the true cause of these tragic events. It examines whether clues should have been found sooner and whether the response to them might have been quicker. Chapter Five draws out general themes which emerge in the chronology, examining in detail the role played by various parties. Chapter Six reviews the recommendations of the Regional Fact Finding Inquiry and Chapter Seven presents our own conclusions and recommendations.

1.12 There will be found in our report many criticisms of things which were done or not done at GKGH, not all of which by any means contributed to the ultimate disaster. It must be remembered that few if any organisations would emerge unscathed from the kind of scrutiny to which we have subjected GKGH. We emphasise that all our expert evidence from independent persons points to the conclusion that a determined and secret criminal may defeat the best regulated organisation in the pursuit of his or her purpose.

CHAPTER TWO: BEVERLY ALLITT

2.1 Introduction

2.1.1   The idea of a nurse deliberately taking the lives of children under her charge is almost unthinkable. Yet this is what the 'Guilty' verdicts against Beverly Allitt force us to accept. At first sight, it might seem extraordinary that someone so inclined could be recruited and trained as a nurse without anyone realising the danger she presented. In this chapter we explore what Allitt was like, and whether anything about her should have warned of the crimes she was later to commit.

2.1.2   We have looked in particular for two possible warning signs. First, whether Allitt's behaviour and attitudes revealed anything unusual about her personality. Secondly, whether there was evidence in her medical history that her attitude to her own health was such that she should not be entrusted with responsibility for the health of others.

2.1.3   A particular reason for considering Allitt's medical history is that it has been suggested that she suffered from Munchausen Syndrome, that is, that she persistently feigned illness and injury, perhaps as a means of gaining attention, either by fabricating symptoms or by harming herself. The suggestion is that this should have been diagnosed, and that the conclusion should have been reached that it made her likely to injure children who would then suffer from the form of abuse which has been called Munchausen Syndrome by Proxy. We consider this proposition in detail in sections 5.3 and 5.4.

2.1.4   Looking back on Allitt's personal and medical history and knowing what she has done, it is tempting to regard everything she did which was out of the ordinary as a clue to the evil she was later to enact on Ward Four. But we must guard against this if our conclusions are to be useful in helping to prevent people with evil intentions from entering the nursing profession. If by excluding people with certain clearly definable characteristics we could be sure of excluding those who might harm vulnerable patients, then it would be worth taking the risk which such a policy would entail of incidentally excluding some people who would have made good nurses. The problem lies in determining which, if any, of Allitt's characteristics are clear indicators of possible danger.

2.2 School

2.2.1   It was during her time at senior school that Beverly Allitt set out on the path which was to lead her into a career in nursing. While she was a pupil at Charles Read School in Corby Glen, she used to babysit regularly for families in the village. She chose 'O' level subjects which pointed her towards a caring career. By the time she left in 1985, it seemed quite natural that her next step should be a pre-nursing course at Grantham College.

2.2.2   It appears that there was nothing remarkable about Allitt as a schoolgirl. Charles Read School is relatively small, with around 230 pupils. Any unusual behaviour would tend to stand out in a school that size. The teaching staff we have interviewed remembered her well, but could not recall any significant incidents in which she was involved which might have caused them to worry about her character.

2.2.3   The teachers found Allitt approachable, and she seemed to get on well with her classmates. She lived in the village and was always willing to help out with events at the school in the evening. She related well to people of different ages, including the younger children in the school. She was not unkind, and showed no signs of ill-temper. Her teachers were aware of her babysitting and never heard any complaints.

2.2.4   The reference provided by the school when Allitt applied to Grantham College described her health as "satisfactory", and a later reference when she applied for training as an enrolled nurse mentioned just one incident when she had injured her arm. Yet she was often seen around the school wearing a bandage or with her arm in a sling. She was known to be accident-prone and suffered from a succession of minor injuries.

2.2.5   We have considered whether Allitt's teachers should have made more of her repeated injuries in the reference they gave her, and in particular whether they should have been suspicious about the causes. The fact is that she was not absent for long periods, and always had a plausible explanation for her injuries. No one had any suspicion that they might not be accidental. She was not the only pupil at the school who was accident-prone, nor the only one to enjoy the attention attracted by a bandage.

2.2.6   We therefore find no grounds on which Allitt's school ought to have discouraged her from her chosen career as a nurse. She was hard-working and dependable, and had shown no signs of dishonesty or cruelty. The only point of interest was her tendency to incur minor injuries. But it is very common to seek attention in this way and a similar tendency can be seen, and was seen at the time, in other teenagers. It is not an indication of secret murderous intent.

2.3 Grantham College

2.3.1   When she left Charles Read School, Beverly Allitt went to Grantham College to attend a pre-nursing course. She could not enter nurse training as she was still too young and had not passed enough 'O' levels to meet the entry requirements. The pre-nursing course gave her the opportunity to take more 'O' levels and to gain some practical experience in a variety of health care settings.

2.3.2   There was a change in Allitt when she moved from school in her small village of Corby Glen to the relatively large town of Grantham for her pre-nursing course.   She found it more difficult to make friends and became shy, quiet and somewhat introverted.   She did not appear to have the ability to reach the academic standard needed to train as a Registered General Nurse.

2.3.3   Allitt's first year tutor noticed that initially she found it difficult on her placements to work with elderly people and mentally handicapped people.   However, her other placements seemed to go well, and over the year she appeared to overcome this initial difficulty.   By the end of the first year, her tutors were pleased with her progress and felt that she had the potential to become a good nurse.

2.3.4   It was during her time at Grantham College that Allitt's injuries and illnesses became more frequent.   She often showed her injuries to her tutors, and appeared to be using them to draw attention to herself.   However, like the school, Grantham College had seen numerous teenagers who exhibited this kind of behaviour and grew out of it.   No one at the college suspected her injuries were self-inflicted.   One of her tutors suspected once that she might have picked at a scratch to make it worse, but she did not doubt the explanation for the original injury.

2.3.5   During her second year, Allitt missed more of the course through sickness, and her sickness absence became a cause for concern.   She was given special permission to take longer over her exams that summer because of an injury to her wrist. Altogether, she missed 52 days out of a possible 180 during her second year and her report at the end of the year indicated that in addition to these absences she had missed lessons while undergoing treatment.   She had missed only eleven days of the first year. The Head of Department wrote in her report, "Clearly Beverly has had a most unsettled year. She may wish to discuss her future when College reconvenes in September".

2.3.6   During her time at Grantham College then, Allitt appears to have been less happy and outgoing than at school. Her health problems were getting worse, but there was still no sign in her general behaviour of what was to come. Certainly none of those who knew her at the time perceived such a sign.

2.4 Recruitment to Nurse Training

2.4.1   Beverly Allitt spent some time back in Corby Glen after the end of her pre-nursing course before applying to train as a nurse. She did not have enough 'O' levels to train as a registered general nurse, so she applied to train for two years as a pupil nurse with a view to becoming an enrolled nurse.

2.4.2   When she applied to South Lincolnshire School of Nursing, as it then was, Allitt did not name a tutor from her pre-nursing course as a referee. Instead, references were provided by her school and a local businessman. This was unusual, especially since some of her work placements had been at GKGH, but the School of Nursing felt they had enough information from the references she gave and from her interview, and did not look further.

2.4.3   The consequence was that Allitt's recent sickness was not brought to the attention of her interviewers at the School of Nursing. She was seen routinely by the Occupational Health nurse on the day of her interview. The only background information available to this nurse was provided by Allitt herself in a standard Declaration of Health form. As she was not aware of any particular cause for concern, the nurse passed her fit for employment as a pupil nurse after the usual examination. We consider the role of Occupational Health in more detail in section 5.5.

2.4.4   We cannot know what the effect on this process would have been if Allitt's recent sickness record had come to light, but it is unfortunate that she found it so easy to conceal. The School of Nursing perhaps failed to recognise that Grantham College might have been able to comment in a reference on such things as attitude to work and attendance record as well as academic ability, which was already attested by her education certificates. We recognise the value of allowing candidates to name their own referees, but **we recommend** that, for all those seeking entry to the nursing profession, in addition to routine references the most recent employer or place of study should be asked to provide at least a record of time taken off on grounds of sickness.

2.4.5   Nevertheless, there was no reason at that time to link Allitt's own health record with the danger she later presented to the children on Ward Four. It seems to us that more robust action over her sickness rate might well have prevented Allitt from becoming a nurse, but this would have been solely because of concern that continuing absences from work would make her an unreliable employee. Had that happened, she would not have had the opportunity to attack the children on Ward Four. It is useless to speculate what she might have done elsewhere.

2.5 Pupil Nurse Training

2.5.1   During the course of her nurse training, Beverly Allitt continued to appear quiet and somewhat lacking in confidence. Her tutors could not recall her being involved in any remarkable incidents. She was an average pupil, and with one exception passed every stage of her studies at the first attempt. The course included ten placements for practical experience on various wards, including one at Pilgrim Hospital in Boston. Reports are not now available on all of Allitt's placements, but we have seen seven, which were generally good. None suggested that her attitude to patients was unusual or uncaring. Once again, the picture we find is of an ordinary girl, who showed no signs of abnormal behaviour or disordered personality.

2.5.2   We ought to mention in passing a series of incidents which occurred in the Nurses' Home while Allitt was in residence. These were episodes of bizarre and often unpleasant behaviour, but we mention them purely because of the coverage they have received in the media. The Assistant General Manager responsible investigated these incidents and drew the conclusion that the perpetrator must be one of a small group of nurses, which included Allitt, or else a former boyfriend of one of them. The group was warned that if the incidents did not stop they would all be evicted from the Nurses' Home. There were no further incidents. This seems to us an entirely appropriate way of dealing with the affair.

2.5.3   We regard this as one of those episodes which takes on a greater significance in retrospect. At the time there was no reason to believe that Allitt, rather than one of the others, was the culprit. Pranks of the kind in question, however malicious, upsetting or even dangerous, are not generally seen as a sign of a murderous character, and rightly so. We do not consider these incidents to be relevant to our Inquiry.

2.5.4   The aspect of Allitt's two years as a pupil nurse which is remarkable is the amount of absence she had through sickness. She missed a total of 126 days during her 110 week course. There is no report in her training records for three of her placements. We have been unable to discover why these reports are missing, but it seems likely that the amount of time she missed during these placements can explain the absence of at least two of them.

2.5.5   Such a high level of sickness was unusual, but in each year there were a handful of students with high sickness rates. Allitt was certainly not alone. While her own training was extended to allow her to make up the days she had missed on the wards, one of her contemporaries missed so much that she was put back a group to repeat a whole section of her training.

2.5.6   Unique or not, we would expect tutors to doubt the suitability for a career in nursing of a pupil nurse who missed 126 days in two years, once again because her attendance might continue to be erratic. It is true that they did commonly take action to discourage random and unnecessary absences. Indeed, early in her training the Senior Tutor interviewed Allitt for this reason. Allitt was able to convince her that her absences were for genuine and various reasons. After the interview her attendance improved for a while, but when she began to have longer absences through sickness these were not followed up.

2.5.7   Allitt's days off were due to a series of unrelated health problems. She had no chronic illness which could be expected to blight her career. We can understand her tutors having sympathy for a pupil who, from their point of view, appeared simply to be having a run of bad luck with her health. Nevertheless, we find it regrettable that, in view of the numerous episodes of sickness, a referral to Occupational Health was not made. This is discussed further in section 5.5.

2.5.8   Although she was never referred by the school, Allitt voluntarily attended the Occupational Health Department at GKGH on 15 occasions during her pupil nurse training and attended the Accident and Emergency Department at GKGH on at least ten occasions. The School of Nursing was not informed of these attendances. But even without this additional information, we regard the time lost through sickness to have been unacceptable and to have required investigation, including discussion with Allitt herself.

2.5.9   Allitt passed her exams to become an enrolled nurse in December 1990, but due to her sickness she had not completed the required number of days' experience on the wards. It was therefore necessary for her to undertake a further ward placement before qualifying as an enrolled nurse.

17

2.5.10   There is no written record of the reasons for the decision to extend Allitt's training and to place her on Ward Four during the extended period. The choice of ward appears to have been made on the basis of Allitt's own preferences and which ward felt able to take an additional student. Her training needs seem to have been disregarded, in particular the fact that she had missed a considerable amount of the required experience on surgical wards. We do not suggest that the first two criteria should be ignored, but we are surprised that the first aim in this case should not have been to fill the gaps which Allitt's absences had left in her general experience.

2.5.11   In our view, it was not appropriate for Allitt to complete her training on Ward Four. Clearly this played a major part in her eventual recruitment as an enrolled nurse on that ward, but she may well have been able to secure a post there anyway. Indeed, had she been placed elsewhere the decision would have had nothing to do with any perceived danger from her. The most we can say is that it contributed to the fact that Ward Four was the location for her crimes.

2.6   Recruitment as an Enrolled Nurse

2.6.1   In December 1990, Beverly Allitt was interviewed in a general recruitment round for GKGH. The hospital tried to ensure that there were enough vacancies for its trainees when they qualified, but did not guarantee them a place if they did not meet the required standard at interview.

2.6.2   These interviews were conducted by a single team on behalf of three of the four clinical service areas of the hospital. This was because Mrs Moira Onions, who was the Clinical Service Manager responsible for Maternity, Gynaecology and Children's Services, had indicated to the other Clinical Service Managers that she had no vacancies in her area. At her interview, Allitt clearly failed to meet the required standard.

18

She showed little interest and very little understanding of how her role would change when she qualified. The decision not to offer her a job was made irrespective of her health record, which was described to us as "appalling".

2.6.3   In February 1991, Allitt was coming to the end of the time she was making up on Ward Four to complete her practical experience. She was due to finish her training on 18th February, but she did not have a job to go to afterwards. Knowing that this was the case and that Allitt was interested in becoming a qualified children's nurse, Mrs Onions made informal enquiries about training courses for her. Mrs Onions' manager was Miss Hannah Newton, the Assistant General Manager responsible for Maternity, Gynaecology and Children's Services. Mrs Onions asked Miss Newton whether there was a course for enrolled nurses to train as Registered Sick Children's Nurses.

2.6.4   Miss Newton made enquiries of the District Nurse Adviser/Director of Nurse Education, Mr Chris Pearce. He advised her that there was such a course in Nottingham, but also that there was a vacancy on the Child Health Branch of the new Project 2000 course at Pilgrim Hospital, Boston, which might be a quicker way of becoming a children's nurse. He suggested she contact the course organiser. Miss Newton passed this on to Mrs Onions and on 13th February 1991 Mrs Onions telephoned Pilgrim Hospital and left a message asking for Allitt to be interviewed with the other candidates later the same day.

2.6.5   The interviewers had no application form or references regarding Beverly Allitt, and they were concerned when they received Mrs Onions' message. Applications for Project 2000 should be made in writing through the Central Clearing House. If an applicant meets the academic criteria and has provided satisfactory references then they may be invited for interview at one of the colleges offering this course. Clearly Allitt had not followed this procedure. The interviewers tried to contact Mrs Onions for more information. Having failed to reach her, they went ahead with Allitt's interview. The way in which this interview was arranged was highly irregular and the more so in view of her sickness record and the fact that she had not yet obtained any practical experience as an enrolled nurse. Following the interview they did not offer her a place.

2.6.6   One of the interviewers at Pilgrim Hospital told us that she telephoned Mrs Onions the following day and told her about the interview. She told her that it had soon become clear that Allitt was not up to the course academically, that she did not appear to be aware of what she was applying for and that she did not seem sure that she wanted a career in paediatrics. Mrs Onions did not recall that conversation. Allitt returned to Ward Four on 14th February somewhat distressed at the prospect of leaving without a job. She told several people that she had been told she would get a place on Project 2000 in September if she first gained six months' experience on a children's ward. This was not true, but it appears to have been accepted by her seniors on Ward Four.

2.6.7   Although Mrs Onions had indicated to the other Clinical Service Managers that she had no vacancies for enrolled nurses in her area, she had been trying for some time to recruit Registered Sick Children's Nurses (RSCNs) to Ward Four. The ward was short of RSCNs, making it difficult to reach the recommended standard of having at least one RSCN on duty at all times. When two RSCNs left Ward Four within weeks of each other shortly before Christmas 1990, there was an urgent need to replace them. We discuss nurse staffing further in section 5.8.

2.6.8   Mrs Onions had advertised for RSCNs nationally and locally in November 1990, but had had no response. Allitt seemed to fit in well with the team on Ward Four and worked hard. It probably seemed to Mrs Onions a pity that she should become unemployed and miss a chance of paediatric experience when she could usefully help out on Ward Four. In view of the shortage of staff, Mrs Onions decided as a short term measure to use funds available for the two vacant posts at different grades to create an enrolled nurse post and agreed to interview Allitt.

2.6.9   Mrs Onions interviewed Allitt on 15th February with Sister Barbara Barker, the ward manager. Mrs Onions holds a Certificate in Personnel Management and on the strength of this she had been allowed to manage the recruitment and appointment of staff to her wards independent of the Personnel Department. She told us that she would not have gone ahead with the interview without references and an application form. Sister Barker could provide one reference herself orally, as Allitt had been working for her, but there is no record of another reference and there is no application form on the file. Sister Barker told us that she did not see an application form. It is unlikely that there would have been anything in either the application form or the other reference to warn of Allitt's criminal tendency, but this points to a lack of rigour in the procedures for her appointment.

2.6.10   Following the interview, Allitt was offered a six-month contract on Ward Four. Sister Barker had been happy with her performance on the ward as a pupil. No reason not to appoint her emerged at the interview. Both Mrs Onions and Sister Barker were aware of the number of days Allitt had been absent through sickness during her training, but Mrs Onions believed that it had been because of an operation. They did not know any more about her medical history and did not consider her attendance record a disqualification. It is not clear to what extent Mrs Onions and Sister Barker were influenced by their false impression that Allitt was likely to start a Project 2000 course in September. The reason given in a memo from Mrs Onions informing the Personnel Department of Allitt's appointment was "to meet the needs of the service". This memo was not sent until 30th May 1991, a matter which we discuss further in paragraph 2.6.15 below.

2.6.11   Allitt began work as an enrolled nurse on Ward Four on 19th February 1991, despite the fact that two important checks had not yet been carried out. First, the offer was subject to satisfactory health screening. Allitt was not screened until 25th February. She was passed fit for employment, but the usual written confirmation of her fitness was not sent to Ward Four until 5th June 1991, by which time she had been arrested and released on police bail. We were unable to obtain a satisfactory explanation for this further irregularity in procedure, although it is doubtful whether it would have made any difference to the course of events.

2.6.12   A second check should have been with the police. Managers are required to check that a candidate has no convictions for criminal offences before appointing them to a post giving substantial access to children[1]. The form requesting this check on Allitt was not completed until after the incidents on Ward Four, but in fact she had no previous convictions.

2.6.13   Allitt's contract could not be signed until these checks were complete and she began to work on Ward Four without a contract. In fact, Occupational Health did not find any reason to reject her on health grounds and, since she had no criminal convictions, it is likely that she would have been appointed whether or not these checks were carried out promptly. Nevertheless, this series of failures to follow normal procedures is extremely worrying. Procedures to prevent unsuitable people from being employed on a children's ward should be rigorously applied.

2.6.14   Virtually none of the procedures in the hospital's recruitment policy was followed when Allitt was appointed. Normally, such matters as the issue and receipt of application forms, requests for references and requests for police checks were handled by the Personnel Department. However, as stated earlier, since Mrs Onions had a Certificate in Personnel

---

[1] See Health Circular HC(88)9, Protection of Children: Disclosure of Criminal Background of those with Access to Children; DHSS 1988.

Management, the Assistant Personnel Manager had delegated these matters to her within her management unit.

2.6.15   Nevertheless, the Personnel Department retained responsibility for issuing a contract and organising induction arrangements for employees recruited by Mrs Onions. They would expect to be informed immediately when someone was offered a post. Even if Mrs Onions failed to inform them, they would expect to be able to tell from changes to the payroll. In the event, the Personnel Department knew nothing of Allitt's appointment until Mrs Onions wrote to inform them on 30th May 1991. The need to authorise the change in Allitt's salary from a pupil nurse to an enrolled nurse was overlooked along with everything else.

2.6.16   All in all, the recruitment of Allitt to Ward Four fell short of standard good practice. We find it disturbing that Mrs Onions apparently failed to realise that she had not completed the process of appointing her, despite being trained to handle personnel matters. We are also concerned that it took so long for the Personnel Department to find out that she had been appointed. Even Mrs Onions' manager, Miss Newton told us that she did not know that an enrolled nurse had been appointed.

2.6.17   As we have said earlier, any close examination of an organisation will reveal some defects in its conduct of affairs. But the facts we have just recounted are symptomatic of a general laxity in GKGH of which we shall give further and more serious examples later. All recruitment procedures are designed to find suitable persons and eliminate unsuitable ones. However, even had everything been done correctly, it is unlikely that Allitt would have been eliminated from the nursing profession.

CHAPTER THREE: THE ATTACKS

3.1 Introduction

3.1.1   In this chapter, we consider the circumstances surrounding the attacks themselves. We now know that between February and April 1991 Beverly Allitt murdered four children and attacked nine others who came to Ward Four for treatment. Some of the children were attacked more than once.

3.1.2   The police were not called in until 30th April 1991. The central question is whether this could and should have happened sooner, thus perhaps preventing some injury and saving some lives. In reviewing the individual cases, we must ask what clues there were that the children were victims of crime rather than suffering unexpected deteriorations in their medical conditions.

3.1.3   In Chapter Four, we review the action, or lack of it, in response to the emerging series of collapses. In this chapter, we consider the circumstances leading to the deaths and injuries of these unfortunate children and the adequacy of the explanations put forward at the time. Although we describe only what happened to the children who became Allitt's victims, one must not forget the background of a busy ward with other patients who did not collapse unexpectedly and in which the cases we describe were, in a sense, submerged.

3.2 Death of Liam James Taylor

3.2.1   On 21st February 1991, just days after Beverly Allitt started work as an enrolled nurse, seven-week-old Liam Taylor was admitted to Ward Four with a severe chest infection. He was admitted under the care of Dr Charith Sena Nanayakkara, one of two Consultant Paediatricians at the hospital. An x-ray showed signs of pneumonia. His condition deteriorated during his stay in hospital, and he needed regular physiotherapy to help him to breathe. By the night of Friday 22nd February he appeared to be beginning to improve slowly.

3.2.2   Allitt was asked to 'special' Liam Taylor, that is, to stay with him constantly to monitor his progress, during the night of Friday 22nd February. Shortly before four o'clock on Saturday morning, the staff nurse in charge of the ward went for her meal break and a charge nurse came to relieve her. Allitt asked both a nursing auxiliary and the charge nurse separately to fetch items of equipment for her. When the Nursing Auxiliary returned she told her that Liam had gone a funny colour. There were red blotches moving over his body, and his breathing was laboured. Liam's condition deteriorated rapidly and the team of doctors and nurses set up to provide emergency resuscitation, usually referred to as the 'crash team', was called.

3.2.3   By 5.30am Liam's heart was beating and he was breathing on a ventilator, but he showed no other signs of life and then began to suffer repeated convulsions. Dr Nanayakkara judged that he had suffered severe brain damage. When he advised Liam's parents of this likelihood, they decided that artificial support should be withdrawn. Liam survived for a few hours, but died later that day.

3.2.4   Exactly what happened to Liam Taylor remains a mystery. The post mortem examination revealed severe damage to his heart muscle, but the pathologist could find no reason why this should have happened. Liam's heart looked like that of an adult who had died of a heart attack (myocardial infarction), yet his arteries and heart showed no signs of pre-existing disease or abnormality. At Allitt's trial, it was the prosecution's case that he had either been suffocated or given a drug which caused his heart to stop.

3.2.5   At the time of Liam's death, Dr Nanayakkara thought that he had collapsed because of his breathing difficulties.

Liam was a very ill baby, but his problems were with his breathing, not with his heart. The pathologist who carried out the post mortem examination was not a paediatric pathologist, and Dr Nanayakkara suspected that such a specialist might have reached a different conclusion. We explore in section 4.2 the steps taken to find a satisfactory explanation for Liam's death. At this stage we note that his sudden death came as a surprise to all those involved in his care, and that the cause was uncertain.

3.3 Death of Timothy William Hardwick

3.3.1   Timothy Hardwick, aged eleven years, suffered from severe cerebral palsy and epilepsy. He was totally dependent on the care of others. On 5th March he was taken to Newark Hospital after having a series of prolonged fits at school. He was given diazepam and transferred to GKGH for observation.

3.3.2   Timothy was admitted to Ward Four later that afternoon. He did not have any more fits and appeared gradually to be recovering from his sedation. At about 5.30pm, Beverly Allitt asked the nurse in charge to come and have a look at Timothy because his breathing was strange. This nurse found him cold and pale, barely breathing and with no heart beat. Doctors spent nearly an hour trying to resuscitate him before confirming that he was dead.

3.3.3   The post mortem report attributed Timothy's death to "status epilepticus", in other words he had stopped breathing as a result of a prolonged series of seizures. However, the nurses said he had not been having fits at the time of his collapse. We find it disturbing that "status epilepticus" was not challenged as a cause of death. We deal with this in section 4.3. As with Liam Taylor, the real cause of Timothy's death is still not known.

3.4 Attacks on Kayley Joanna Desmond

3.4.1   Fourteen-month-old Kayley Desmond was already a patient on Ward Four when Timothy Hardwick died. She was being treated for a lower respiratory tract infection. In the early hours of Sunday 10th March, while Beverly Allitt was attending to her, Kayley suddenly stopped breathing. Allitt wrote in her nursing notes, "Began to cough - then suddenly had respiratory arrest". By the time the emergency resuscitation team arrived Kayley was breathing again. An hour later she was stable and the doctors left the room, only to be called back a few minutes later when she stopped breathing again.

3.4.2   Allitt, who had been present during both these collapses, was asked to stay with Kayley for the rest of the night. A nurse from elsewhere in the hospital was asked to come to Ward Four to share this responsibility. At about 4.00am, Kayley arched her back and stopped breathing again. Following this third attack, Kayley was transferred to Queen's Medical Centre in Nottingham, where she made a rapid recovery. She was transferred back to GKGH on Tuesday, 12th March.

3.4.3   Kayley Desmond was born with a cleft palate, and had always had trouble feeding. Combined with her chest infection, it was thought that this had caused her to vomit some milk and inhale it, which in turn caused her breathing to stop. After the first collapse Dr Nanayakkara, the Consultant Paediatrician responsible for her treatment, wrote, "Cause? Not clear", then below, "Aspiration". This was a reasonable explanation based on the facts which were known at the time. Subsequently closer examination of x-rays taken both at GKGH and at Queen's Medical Centre suggested a different cause. This is discussed further in section 4.4.

27

3.5 Attacks on Paul Ashley Crampton

3.5.1   On Wednesday, 20th March 1991, five-month-old Paul Crampton was admitted to Ward Four with a history of wheezing. He was diagnosed as suffering from either a mild to moderate chest infection or mild asthma. He responded well to treatment and plans were made to discharge him on the following Sunday.

3.5.2   However, on the Saturday afternoon, the nurses who came to give Paul his routine drug treatment, one of whom was Beverly Allitt, found that he was cold and clammy. He was showing all the signs of hypoglycaemia, or low blood sugar, although he was not diabetic and had been fed recently. He was put on a glucose drip and recovered. On the Sunday morning the drip was taken down. Later that morning, Paul's father found him cold and clammy again. A bedside test on his blood indicated that his blood sugar was probably very low again. Later a blood sample was taken and tested in the laboratory. The result confirmed that Paul's blood glucose was low.

3.5.3   Paul recovered once more when the glucose drip was restored. He had no further attacks over the next few days, and the amount of glucose infused was gradually reduced. Paul's third hypoglycaemic episode occurred on Thursday, 28th March, the day Allitt returned to the ward after three days off duty. Following this episode Paul was transferred to Queen's Medical Centre where he underwent further investigation and gradually recovered.

3.5.4   Dr Nelson Porter, the Consultant Paediatrician in charge of Paul's treatment, could not understand why his blood sugar kept dropping so dramatically. He considered various explanations and took steps to investigate whether they were correct. He ordered a blood sample to be taken on Monday, 25th March, and insisted that the insulin level be measured although Paul's blood sugar was normal when it was taken. He also sent off another sample of Paul's blood, taken after he collapsed again on 28th March, for measurement of insulin. It should be noted that Dr Porter ordered these tests because he thought Paul might be suffering from a condition which caused his body to produce too much insulin, a fact to which we will refer later.

3.6   Attack on Bradley John Gibson

3.6.1   On 29th March, the day after Paul Crampton was transferred to Nottingham, five-year-old Bradley Gibson was admitted to Ward Four because he could not keep down the antibiotics his General Practitioner had prescribed for a chest infection. An intravenous drip was set up to give him the antibiotics. During the night, Bradley complained twice that his arm was hurting where the drip was attached. On both occasions, it was Beverly Allitt who went to check his drip site.

3.6.2   Soon after Allitt went to him the second time, Bradley suddenly slumped forward. Another nurse joined Allitt and they found that he wasn't breathing and had no pulse. The 'crash team' was called, but it took more than half an hour to revive Bradley. He was put on a ventilator and, as soon as he was stabilised, he was transferred to Queen's Medical Centre.

3.6.3   Bradley remained on the ventilator for three days in Nottingham. His recovery was complicated by neurological problems thought to be a result of the prolonged cardiac arrest, but he had no further problems with his heart and examination ruled out any underlying abnormality of his heart. His neurological condition improved gradually, and he was discharged from Nottingham on 19th April.

3.7   Attacks on Yik Hung 'Henry' Chan

3.7.1   Two-year-old Yik Hung Chan had a history of asthma and eczema for which he had previously been treated on Ward Four.

29

He was known on the ward as Henry. He had been admitted on 28th March after falling out of an upstairs window, which resulted in a fracture of his skull. He vomited frequently during his first few days in hospital, but the vomiting gradually ceased. On Sunday 31st March, he was well enough to play with his mother. At nine o'clock that evening, Beverly Allitt called the other nursing staff to come and see Henry because he was crying. They could not hear him, and when they got there they found Henry blue, with his back arched. Several pillows were on the bed.

3.7.2   Henry was given oxygen and soon he began breathing again. The episode was diagnosed as a febrile convulsion. Henry's temperature was indeed raised, but none of the nurses who observed the episode agreed that what they had seen was a typical febrile convulsion. Allitt was left alone with Henry once more, and about an hour later she raised the alarm again. Again, Henry was blue, stiff and his back was arched. He recovered quickly.

3.7.3   Henry was transferred that night to Queen's Medical Centre. The working diagnosis was that he was suffering from fits either as a result of his head injury or because of his very high temperature. Henry did not have any more fits and he was discharged on 5th April after his condition had improved and his temperature had returned to normal. The doctors in Nottingham could not be certain what had caused his fits, but they were reassured by his recovery.

3.8   Death of Becky Grace Phillips

3.8.1   Becky Phillips was one of twin baby sisters born prematurely. Both twins had spent a lot of time in hospital since their birth on 31st January 1991. Becky was discharged from Ward Four on 4th April after treatment for vomiting and diarrhoea. Beverly Allitt fed her at midday, and another nurse fed her shortly before she was discharged at 4.00pm. During the evening at home, Becky showed unusual signs of discomfort. Her parents called out their family doctor, who advised them that Becky had no more than severe colic.

3.8.2   Becky settled for a while, but woke during the night and still did not seem well. Mr and Mrs Phillips took her into their own bed at quarter to three in the morning. Fifteen minutes later they woke to find that she had stopped breathing. They tried to resuscitate her themselves and rushed her to the hospital, but efforts to revive her failed.

3.8.3   No reason for Becky's death could be found in the post mortem examination or on routine biochemical analyses, so it was concluded that it was a Cot Death. For this reason, a blood sample was taken shortly after her death for later analysis. When suspicions about the events on Ward Four were being investigated, this sample was tested for insulin. The result of this test showed that Becky had been injected with a large quantity of insulin. The reasons why this test was not carried out sooner are explored in Chapter Four.

3.9 Attacks on Katie Sue Phillips

3.9.1   Following Becky's sudden unexplained death, her twin sister Katie was admitted to Ward Four as a precaution. She was quite well when she was examined on the morning of Friday, 5th April, just hours after her sister had died. That afternoon, while Beverly Allitt was allocated to 'special' her, she suddenly stopped breathing. She recovered quickly, but then on Sunday it happened again. This time it took longer to restart her breathing and she began to have fits. At six o'clock she stopped breathing again and her heart stopped beating. It took a long time to restart her heart. It was discovered that air was leaking from her lungs into the chest cavity, a situation which required urgent and expert attention. The condition, known as pneumothorax, could have been a side-effect of vigorous resuscitation. As soon as Katie was stable she was transferred to Nottingham City Hospital.

3.9.2   Several tests had already been carried out in Grantham to discover whether some virus or other infection might have affected both twins.   These investigations were continued in Nottingham, and the doctors also considered whether there might have been a metabolic cause. All of these tests proved negative. Katie continued to have fits, but she recovered well and was gradually allowed to breathe unaided.   On 16th April she was transferred back to GKGH.   The discharge letter concluded, "Despite extensive investigations, we do not have a reason for Katie to be so unwell at the same time as her sister".   As with Kayley Desmond, closer examination of a series of x-rays taken during Katie's stay in hospital later provided a clue to the true reason, which we discuss further in section 4.9.

3.10 Attack on Michael Darren Davidson

3.10.1   Later in the evening of Sunday, 7th April 1991, a six-year-old boy named Michael Davidson was admitted to GKGH having been shot accidentally in the stomach with an air gun.   He underwent an operation that evening to have a pellet removed and was taken to Ward Four to recover.   Two days later, Beverly Allitt helped a doctor to prepare the dose of an antibiotic which Michael had been receiving since the operation.   While the doctor was administering the drug intravenously, Michael's limbs stiffened and he became blue around the mouth.   The doctor could not feel him breathing.   Gradually, Michael's heart stopped beating.

3.10.2   Michael came round quite quickly when doctors began to resuscitate him.   Dr Nanayakkara, who was on the ward when it happened, concluded that Michael had been overbreathing and that this had led to a kind of fit.   A blood sample was taken and analysed that day.   It did not show the low calcium level which might have accompanied such an episode.   This puzzled Dr Nanayakkara, but he told us that the surgeons and anaesthetists who were in charge of Michael's treatment told him that what had happened was not unknown in children recovering from an operation. Michael had no further problems and was discharged home on 12th April.

3.11 Attacks on Christopher William Steven Peasgood

3.11.1   Seven-week-old Christopher Peasgood was admitted to Ward Four with a chest infection on Friday 12th April. He was very ill and needed oxygen. During the afternoon of the following day he suddenly stopped breathing and went blue. He was resuscitated and recovered gradually. He was monitored closely for the rest of the day.

3.11.2   At about twenty to eight that evening, Beverly Allitt took over from the nurse who was staying with Christopher, to give her a short break. Christopher's parents had also left to get something to eat. Just minutes after being left alone with Christopher, Allitt raised the alarm. He was blue in the face. His heart rate was high and he was not getting enough oxygen into his blood. He responded to treatment again and was transferred to Queen's Medical Centre soon afterwards. There he made a rapid recovery and was discharged home on 16th April.

3.11.3   Two possible explanations for Christopher's collapse were explored. First, it was thought he might have inhaled some milk and choked. Alternatively, it was possible that his existing breathing problems had deteriorated to a point where he could not maintain the proper level of oxygen in his blood. But tests of his oxygen and carbon dioxide levels did not support this. Another explanation consistent with the signs recorded is that he was suffocated.

3.12 Attacks on Christopher John King

3.12.1   Christopher King was born in March 1991.   He experienced some breathing difficulties following his birth. When he was a month old he began vomiting repeatedly and was admitted to Ward Four to determine the cause.   There was a curious incident a few days later when he became grey, but he recovered quickly with oxygen.   On the next day, Monday 15th April, the cause of his vomiting was identified as a pyloric stenosis, which is a narrowing of the muscular outlet of the stomach.   An operation to correct this was performed that evening.

3.12.2   The following morning Beverly Allitt, who had found Christopher when he went grey, was again allocated to look after him.   At eight o'clock she raised the alarm: Christopher had become blue and had more or less stopped breathing. He was given emergency treatment and his condition improved.   A short time later, Allitt came out of the room he was in to say that it had happened again.   Once again he recovered quickly.

3.12.3   At 10.30am the doctors were called back again. Christopher was having difficulty breathing and had become blue again.   It had been thought that the previous episodes were caused by him inhaling his own vomit, but tests and x-rays this time showed that that was not the case. Neither the Paediatric Consultant nor the Consultant Surgeon who had performed Christopher's operation was able to say why it had happened, so it was decided to transfer him to Queen's Medical Centre.   The staff there found no medical explanation for his attacks.   He suffered no further attacks during his stay in Nottingham.

3.13 Attacks on Patrick Robert Elstone

3.13.1   On 16th April 1991, seven-week-old twin Patrick Elstone was ill at home.   He developed diarrhoea and he became dehydrated, lethargic and did not feed well. His General Practitioner decided he should be taken to hospital and Patrick was admitted to Ward Four where a diagnosis of possible gastroenteritis was made. Two days later, although he was not very ill, Patrick was isolated because tests had identified an infection which might be passed on to other patients. Later that afternoon Beverly Allitt asked the staff nurse in charge of the ward to look at Patrick. She found him pale and grey with very shallow breathing. He recovered with oxygen. There was no apparent reason why this episode should have happened, so the nurses decided to observe him more closely.

3.13.2   Patrick appeared to improve during the evening and the nurse who had been allocated to keep an eye on him began to leave him for longer periods while she cared for other patients. At eight o'clock she was with another patient when Allitt came out of Patrick's cubicle to report that he was blue and not breathing. He was given emergency treatment to resuscitate him and recovered after about ten minutes. No medical explanation for his collapse was found. He was transferred to Queen's Medical Centre for further treatment.

3.14 Death of Claire Louise Peck

3.14.1   Claire Peck had been a patient on Ward Four several times since her birth in January 1990 before what was to be her final admission on Monday 22nd April 1991. She had been on the ward for a few days the previous week with suspected asthma, and on that Monday she suffered an asthma attack at home and was brought back to hospital. Treatment was started, but Claire continued to wheeze, although without signs of her condition deteriorating.

3.14.2   Claire was taken into the Treatment Room so that an intravenous drip could be set up. Beverly Allitt was left watching her while preparations were made. When another nurse returned to the room, Claire was dark blue, rigid and was not breathing. She was given oxygen through a face mask and soon began breathing again.

3.14.3   Claire was given a drug for her asthma and seemed to be improving, but an hour later Allitt raised the alarm again. Claire was dark blue and was not breathing. The other nurses and the Consultant, Dr Porter returned to the room just as her heart stopped beating. The team made vigorous attempts to resuscitate her. They were successful in restoring circulation and oxygen saturation of the blood, but her heart still would not restart. Claire was declared dead later that evening.

CHAPTER FOUR: THE RESPONSE TO THE ATTACKS

4.1 Introduction and Background

4.1.1   In this chapter we will explore the action which was taken in response to each of the episodes described in Chapter Three. We will consider what led to the eventual conclusion that someone was deliberately harming the children, and whether that conclusion could or should have been reached sooner.

4.1.2   Some background information on GKGH, and the paediatric service in particular, will be helpful in considering this question. The area served by GKGH has a population of just under 100,000, with approximately 30,000 children. The number of births annually is about 2,250. Sixty per cent of these babies are born at GKGH.

4.1.3   At the beginning of 1991, twenty beds were available for children requiring medical or surgical treatment on Ward Four.   Nine of these beds were for patients of the two Consultant Paediatricians, Dr F N Porter and Dr C S Nanayakkara, and the remainder for patients of other specialists. On average, twelve of the beds were occupied at a time. Between 1986 and 1989, no child died on Ward Four. In 1990, an eleven day old baby and a seven year old girl died on the ward. In view of the seriousness of their conditions, the death of neither of these children was unexpected.

4.1.4   When children on Ward Four needed highly specialised treatment or intensive care, which the ward was neither staffed nor equipped to give them, they were transferred to one of the specialist children's units in Nottingham. This was not a frequent occurrence, and many of the transfers were planned for specific operations or investigations which could not be carried out in Grantham. Three children were transferred in the first four months of 1990, and in the equivalent period in 1989 there were only two transfers.

4.1.5   Against this background, we review in this chapter what clues there were at the time and later as to what had actually happened to Beverly Allitt's victims. We consider what action was taken to explore these clues. As ever we have tried to set aside the effect of retrospection, which magnifies and distorts fragments of information which are now known to be crucial but the significance of which was not realised at the time. Nevertheless, we have sought to investigate fully the reasons for these failures to recognise the emerging pattern.

4.2 Liam Taylor

4.2.1   Liam Taylor's sudden deterioration came as a surprise to all those involved in his care. A few babies die each year of severe respiratory infections, but usually they deteriorate gradually before finally succumbing. Dr Nanayakkara was puzzled by the sudden change in Liam's condition, and by the fact that it took a long time to resuscitate him after the initial collapse. He therefore sought and obtained the permission of Liam's parents for a post mortem examination, which he assured them would be undertaken by a paediatric pathologist.

4.2.2   A death certificate was issued before the post mortem, giving the cause of Liam's death as pneumonia with probable septicaemia.   The Registrar was by law unable to accept septicaemia as a cause of death, so a Coroner's post mortem was ordered.   Dr Nanayakkara had intended a paediatric pathologist to carry out the hospital post mortem he had requested. He told us that when he heard on 25th February that his request had been superseded by a Coroner's post mortem, he telephoned the Coroner's Officer and the Grantham pathologist, who usually carried out post mortem examinations on behalf of the Coroner. He tried to persuade them that a paediatric pathologist should conduct the autopsy, but his request was refused by both.

4.2.3   The pathologist, Dr Terry Marshall, who was a locum, told us that his impression was that Dr Nanayakkara telephoned because he was sure that the cause of Liam's death was pneumonia and he objected strongly to the decision to hold a Coroner's post mortem. Although Dr Marshall confirmed that Dr Nanayakkara had asked for a paediatric pathologist to be engaged, he indicated that Dr Nanayakkara seemed greatly upset and that he made out no case to support this request.

4.2.4   On the other hand, the Coroner's Officer, Mr Maurice Stonebridge-Foster, actually denied that any request that a paediatric pathologist should conduct the post mortem was made by Dr Nanayakkara on 25th February 1991. He stated that Dr Nanayakkara did telephone the mortuary on that day, but that the call came after the post mortem had been completed and that its purpose was to try to persuade Dr Marshall to change the cause of death on the report to the Coroner from 'myocardial infarction' to 'pneumonia', which was his own diagnosis. He stated that Dr Nanayakkara did request that a second post mortem should be carried out, this time by a paediatric pathologist, but that his request by telephone came over a week later, by which time Liam's body had been removed from the mortuary.

4.2.5   After the passing of nearly three years, it would be no surprise to find honest lapses of recollection among witnesses. But alone among those concerned, Dr Nanayakkara made contemporaneous notes of the course of events, which we have no reason to disbelieve. And his records clearly support his evidence to us that he did ask for a post mortem examination by a paediatric pathologist on the day which he recorded as 25th February and that it was refused by both the persons to whom he made the request, namely Dr Marshall and Mr Stonebridge-Foster.

4.2.6   On the balance of probabilities we are satisfied that Dr Nanayakkara's recollection, assisted by his contemporaneous notes, is correct. We prefer it to the confusing and incompatible recollections of the other witnesses on this point,

39

unsupported by any notes with which to refresh their memories. Dr Nanayakkara had no motive at the time for recording these matters other than accurately.

4.2.7   Furthermore, we are satisfied that the formal decision not to instruct a paediatric pathologist was made by Mr Stonebridge-Foster. The Coroner himself, Mr T J Pert, told us that he was not informed of Dr Nanayakkara's request. He went on to say that the Grantham pathologist had authority to bring in a specialist pathologist if necessary. He believed that Dr Marshall was aware of this, but Dr Marshall told us that he was not aware of any such authority and that it was for the Coroner's Officer, acting on behalf of the Coroner, to decide who should carry out the autopsy. We find it regrettable that Dr Marshall and Mr Stonebridge-Foster rejected Dr Nanayakkara's request, which was reasonable in the circumstances. This rejection was the more regrettable in the light of the subsequent findings of a paediatric pathologist, Dr David Fagan, which we discuss below.

4.2.8   Dr Marshall's post mortem findings were highly unusual. Liam Taylor's heart was damaged in a similar way to the heart of an adult who had suffered a myocardial infarction, which is damage to the heart muscle usually due to blockage of an artery. Liam's arteries were in fact clear. Dr Marshall had never seen a similar pattern of damage in a child's heart. Histology revealed no explanation. He wrote to Mr Pert that Liam had died of a myocardial infarction, but that the cause of this was "a medical mystery". Despite this, Mr Pert accepted myocardial infarction as a cause of death and Liam's death certificate was signed. We were very surprised to learn that Mr Pert did not see it as his role to seek a solution to this "medical mystery". However, we also note that in the same letter Dr Marshall stated clearly that despite his doubts, "in the absence of any indication to the contrary, I must presume this to be a natural death".

4.2.9   Despite his persistent requests, Dr Nanayakkara did not receive a copy of the post mortem report until 3rd April 1991. Neither Mr Pert nor Dr Marshall was able to tell us why he was not sent a copy sooner. Mr Pert told us he was sure that post mortem reports were usually sent to the consultant involved, but he gave no grounds for so thinking. Dr Marshall could not recall whether they were or not, but he believed that it was the Coroner's responsibility anyway. In our view, it is for the Coroner to determine who else should receive the report and to ensure that copies are sent, since the report is made to him and is his property. **We recommend** that in every case Coroners should send copies of post mortem reports to any consultant who has been involved in the patient's care prior to death, whether or not demanded under Rule 57 of the Coroner's Rules 1984.

4.2.10   When Dr Nanayakkara found out that Dr Marshall had concluded that Liam had died of a myocardial infarction, he found it difficult to accept. Such happenings are virtually unheard of in children with no pre-existing disease or abnormality of the heart and Liam had neither. Dr Marshall himself found it difficult to accept; he searched widely in books and journals for an explanation, but he found nothing. Dr Nanayakkara and Dr Marshall each met Liam's parents and told them that they had no explanation to offer for the damage to Liam's heart.

4.2.11   Dr Nanayakkara continued to press for a second post mortem to be carried out by a paediatric pathologist. He contacted Dr David Fagan, a Consultant Paediatric Pathologist on the Home Office list, to see if he would be prepared to carry out the examination. He was apparently unaware that Dr Marshall had already consulted Dr Fagan and given him some slides. Dr Fagan asked Dr Marshall to send him further specimens.

4.2.12   On 24th March, Dr Nanayakkara wrote to Mr Pert expressing his concerns about Liam Taylor and asking for a copy of the post mortem report, which he had still not received. He asked whether a paediatric pathologist might be instructed in similar cases. Mr Pert received this letter on the same day as a letter from Dr Marshall, who had received a copy of Dr Nanayakkara's letter and was writing to respond to the implied criticism of himself. Dr Marshall agreed that a specialist would be better than a generalist for any particular specialty, but in defending his original findings he did not concede that a paediatric pathologist might have been able to shed further light on Liam's particular case.

4.2.13   The Coroner told us that Dr Marshall's letter led him to believe that the two men had discussed the matter and that he need not reply to Dr Nanayakkara's letter. However, the letter plainly called for an answer in our view, asking as it did specific questions which remain unanswered to this day. We have learned in the course of our Inquiry that a paediatric pathologist is now always brought in to conduct autopsies on children in Grantham as a matter of routine, but that does not excuse what is at the very least a lack of courtesy in what was a mysterious and distressing situation.

4.2.14   On 9th April 1991, Dr Marshall's locum appointment at GKGH came to an end and he left to take up an appointment in Australia. Shortly before he left, he sent to Dr Fagan further specimens taken from Liam's heart. Again, Dr Nanayakkara appears to have been unaware of this. He wrote to Dr Marshall on 17th April asking for a paediatric pathologist to be asked for a second opinion. The specimens Dr Fagan had received were not sufficient on their own for him to form an immediate judgment as to the cause of Liam's death. It was not until the police provided him with further specimens in June, and with typed medical notes and x-rays in relation to all the children in July, that Dr Fagan was able to exclude a natural explanation.

4.2.15   When he produced his report for the police, Dr Fagan confirmed that there was severe myocardial damage, but he could find no evidence of any primary disease which could have produced it. In the light of the information available in December 1991, when he wrote his report, he concluded that the cause of death was administration of a noxious substance. He sought a second opinion from Professor John Emery, Emeritus Professor of Paediatric Pathology at Sheffield University. Professor Emery also concluded that the cause of Liam's death was not natural.

4.2.16   We cannot tell what Dr Fagan's conclusion would have been if he had carried out the initial post mortem examination. In fact he was never able to conduct a full autopsy himself, since Liam's body had been cremated. His principal finding, on the basis of the samples, records and photographs he did examine, was severe myocardial damage with no apparent cause, which was not dissimilar to that of Dr Marshall. But he told us in evidence that when confronted with pathological findings that he could not explain, he made it his business to go back over all the available clinical evidence prior to death in consultation with those who had cared for the patient. We cannot eliminate the possibility that, if everything had been done as it ought to have been, the first clue that there had been criminal activity might have emerged at this early stage. In particular, **we recommend** that the provision of paediatric pathology services be reviewed with a view to ensuring that such services be engaged in every case in which the death of a child is unexpected or clinically unaccountable, whether the post mortem examination is ordered by a Coroner or requested in routine hospital practice.

4.2.17   By 5th March, then, Dr Nanayakkara knew little more about the cause of Liam Taylor's death than he did ten days earlier. He was continuing to pursue it, but at this stage he had no reason to suspect that Liam had been the victim of an attack. Nevertheless, he was clearly concerned by it.

4.3 **Timothy Hardwick**

4.3.1   Timothy Hardwick died within three hours of admission to hospital, so Dr Nanayakkara was unable to issue a death certificate and a Coroner's post mortem was ordered. Once more it was Dr Marshall who carried out the post mortem examination. He recorded multiple small haemorrhages in the lungs which, he stated, were characteristic, although not diagnostic, of an asphyxial type of death and "virtually exactly as would be expected from a death in status epilepticus".

4.3.2   The cause of death was recorded as: 1a) status epilepticus; and 1b) cerebral palsy. Our understanding is that the term "status epilepticus", indicating a succession of fits without intermission, describes a clinical condition rather than a pathological diagnosis, and the recorded history prior to death suggests that Timothy was not in fact in status epilepticus. Nevertheless, Dr Marshall told us that he gave "status epilepticus" as a cause of death, knowing that Timothy had suffered from epilepsy and being satisfied that there was no unnatural cause. It should be noted that Timothy did not live in Grantham and he had received specialist treatment in Nottingham, so he was not well known on Ward Four. The Consultant in Mental Handicap from Nottingham who had been involved in his long-term care did not raise any queries about his dying in this way.

4.3.3   By 6th March, then, there had been two unexpected deaths on Ward Four. This was very unusual and we would expect exploration of their causes to have continued, as indeed it did. But until and unless such exploration yielded some common factor, there was no special reason to connect the two deaths. The two cases were very different. Liam Taylor was a previously healthy small baby, whereas Timothy Hardwick was a severely handicapped 11 year old boy. One was in hospital with a chest infection, the other following epileptic fits. At this stage, Dr Nanayakkara believed that both suffered heart failure as a result of respiratory arrests, from quite different causes. Two unexpected deaths on the ward so close together could reasonably be regarded as an unlucky coincidence.

44

4.4 Kayley Desmond

4.4.1   Beverly Allitt's next victim was Kayley Desmond. Given the fact that she had a cleft palate, it was not unreasonable to conclude that Kayley's collapse had been caused by inhalation of vomit. But in this case, something which was to prove a vital clue at Allitt's trial was overlooked at the time. An x-ray was taken after the second attack. It showed not only the changes in the lungs associated with pneumonia, but also pockets of what appeared to be air in her right upper arm and armpit.

4.4.2   With modern equipment for giving intravenous infusions, it is extremely unlikely that air could have entered Kayley's body accidentally in the course of her treatment. If the air had leaked from her lungs, it should have been visible on both sides and would have been more likely to have tracked up her neck than into her arm. Therefore, if this observation had been made at the time, the possibility would have had to be envisaged that air had entered as a result of some improper interference. We cannot know what conclusions would have been reached. At the least, it is possible that this clue, added to the other fragments of evidence which later emerged, would have contributed to the pressure to think the unthinkable, and might have caused Allitt to be stopped earlier.

4.4.3   This air was also visible on a further x-ray taken at Queen's Medical Centre (QMC). The question which at once arises is why the air in Kayley's armpit was not observed when these x-rays were examined at the time. It was not in fact observed on either film until the Consultant Paediatric Radiologist at QMC was asked by the police to review all the x-rays.

4.4.4   Both x-rays were taken to help the doctors to monitor the progress of Kayley's chest infection. The film taken on the ward in Grantham was sent to the Radiology Department there after Kayley returned from Nottingham. A written report on the findings was sent to Ward Four on 22nd March. The air was not observed. The late reporting was largely due to the fact that the film had gone to Nottingham with Kayley. No radiology report appears on the file of Kayley's medical records at QMC. It appears that, rather than sending the x-ray to be examined by a radiologist, the doctors relied on their own judgment. Although the usual practice was to send x-ray films to be reported in the Radiology Department after they had been reviewed on the ward, it appears that this did not happen in this case. If the films were sent to the Radiology Department, as we believe they should have been, they were certainly not reported.

4.4.5   We have ourselves seen both these x-rays and can confirm that the air is not immediately obvious, but it can be seen clearly with a bright light. We are not surprised that the doctors, looking mainly at Kayley's lungs and concerned with the immediate care of this very sick child, did not give the x-rays the careful scrutiny needed to detect the air in Kayley's armpit. But radiologists are trained to scan the whole picture. It is unfortunate that the more specialised paediatric radiologists in Nottingham were not asked to review the second x-ray. We consider that best practice should include the scrutiny of all x-rays by a radiologist and the production of a written report.

4.5 Paul Crampton

4.5.1   It was the sample of Paul Crampton's blood which Dr Porter took on 28th March which eventually gave the first clear evidence that something untoward was happening on Ward Four. The laboratory at GKGH is not equipped to measure insulin levels, the measurement of which requires a sophisticated hormone assay. Samples are sent away for testing at one of the five specialist laboratories which provide this service to the whole country. The samples which were taken on 25th March and 28th March were sent to the Supraregional Assay Service Laboratories at the Hammersmith Hospital in London and the University Hospital of Wales in Cardiff respectively.

46

4.5.2   Insulin is a hormone, or chemical messenger, which controls the way the body uses glucose. If the body does not produce sufficient insulin then the amount of glucose in the blood rises. This is what can happen in untreated cases of diabetes. Many diabetic patients require to be treated with insulin by injection. On the other hand, if there is too much insulin then the blood glucose level falls, leading to what is called hypoglycaemia (too little sugar in the blood). This in turn can lead to coma and even severe brain damage, sometimes resulting in death. In rare cases hypoglycaemia can be due to a tumour in the pancreas which causes the body to produce too much insulin.

4.5.3   Insulin which is introduced into the body from an external source is usually referred to as 'exogenous' insulin, to distinguish it from 'endogenous' insulin produced in the body. When insulin is formed naturally in the body, a substance known as c-peptide is produced as a by-product. Since c-peptide disappears from the blood much more slowly than insulin, when the insulin is endogenous the blood always contains a proportion of c-peptide to insulin which remains more or less constant. This is true even when there is an insulin-secreting pancreatic tumour. When hypoglycaemia is induced by the administration of 'exogenous' insulin, the level of c-peptide remains low.

4.5.4   Paul Crampton was not hypoglycaemic when the sample of his blood was taken on 25th March although his blood sugar had become very low several times over the previous weekend. The result of the insulin assay on this sample was not available until 13th May 1991, but it would have revealed only a modest elevation of the insulin level. The level was not outside the range expected in a patient receiving an intravenous infusion of glucose, as Paul was when the sample was taken. The sample was not tested for c-peptide.

4.5.5   The sample taken on 28th March, which was sent for testing in Cardiff, contained so much insulin that it was beyond the range of the equipment used to measure it. Very low levels of c-peptide were found. These results provided conclusive evidence that Paul had been given 'exogenous' insulin.

4.5.6   The weekend following Thursday 28th March 1991 was Easter weekend. Both Friday 29th March and Monday 1st April were therefore Bank Holidays. For this reason, the sample of Paul Crampton's blood taken on 28th March was not sent off to Cardiff until Tuesday 2nd April. It arrived in Cardiff on 4th April, but was not tested until 12th April. The results were reported to Dr Porter by telephone as soon as they had been confirmed.

4.5.7   We heard evidence from the staff of the Supraregional Assay Service Laboratories at Cardiff. Samples received there are 'batched', that is to say, accumulated until the number awaiting analysis is sufficient to make the setting up of the assay, a laborious and expensive procedure, economically worthwhile. A lapse of up to eight days is therefore quite usual and in most cases is not significant from the clinical point of view. However, if the Laboratories are notified by telephone or otherwise that there is a special need to have the earliest possible results of the test, they will set up the analysis 'ad hoc'. It is not sufficient merely to write "Urgent" on the bottle: as the witnesses observed, "everyone is liable to do that", and it defeats its own purpose. We have found no reason to criticise the Cardiff laboratories. On the contrary, when they found the level of insulin in Paul Crampton's blood was very high indeed and the c-peptide level was low, they correctly saw the significance of the finding and telephoned Dr Porter in Grantham late on a Friday afternoon to tell him urgently what they had found.

4.5.8   We have, however, asked ourselves whether Dr Porter should have requested the Assay Service to make a special and urgent examination of the blood sample from Paul Crampton. Once again, it would be easy to judge his action or inaction in the light of what we know now. But Dr Porter requested an analysis

48

not because he suspected that Paul Crampton had been given insulin exogenously, but because he thought Paul might have had an insulin-producing tumour in his pancreas, a rare but not unknown condition in children. This is an important observation to make, but not a reason for demanding priority over all the other samples awaiting analysis. Nor was the delay in getting the sample to Cardiff culpable in the light of the same considerations. On the other hand, from the moment that Dr Porter received news of the analysis from Cardiff the situation was profoundly different and we shall consider later his response to that information.

4.6 Bradley Gibson

4.6.1   While Paul Crampton's blood sample was waiting its turn to be tested, other events were occurring in Grantham. On 30th March, Bradley Gibson collapsed and was transferred to Queen's Medical Centre. A number of points in the history of Bradley Gibson's sudden collapse suggest that it might have been caused by a drug which disrupted his heart rhythm. Bradley's complaints of soreness in his arm at the site of his drip, his sudden loss of consciousness and the fact that it took thirty-two minutes to restore a normal heart beat are all consistent with the later hypothesis that potassium had been added to his infusion fluid. A blood sample taken at 4.15am, about an hour after his heart stopped, was tested at GKGH and the results reported on Tuesday 2nd April. The level of potassium was 6.2 mmol/L, compared to a normal range of 3.7 to 5.0 mmol/L.

4.6.2   Potassium is essential to the working of the body, but if someone is given too much potassium, it can disrupt the heart rhythm and in large doses it can even cause the heart to stop beating. According to some witnesses, concentrations of potassium above 6.0 mmol/L may be sufficient to have toxic effects on the heart. However, it is possible that the high concentration of potassium in Bradley Gibson's blood could be explained by the fact that the blood sample was taken after his prolonged period of cardiac arrest, which can cause the blood to become more acidic and raise the concentration of potassium.

4.6.3   Whatever the actual cause of Bradley's collapse, it is clear that the doctors involved in his care, both at Grantham and at Nottingham, could not explain it. Dr Porter thought the cause might have been some abnormality of Bradley's heart muscle, but tests in Nottingham excluded this. The doctors in Nottingham did not think it could have been caused by his respiratory problems. This extraordinary case, coming so soon after Paul Crampton's transfer to Nottingham, should have raised questions.

4.6.4   This was the seventh unusual and unexpected episode of collapse of a child on Ward Four within a period of about four weeks. There did not seem to be any clinical reason to make a connection between the previous collapses and that of Bradley Gibson. There was no suspicion of hypoglycaemia in respect of any of the children other than Paul Crampton. Yet the cumulative effect on a thinking person ought to have been, in our judgment, to force a close and anxious scrutiny of all seven episodes. Matters had progressed beyond the bounds of reasonable expectation. Indeed, Dr Porter was compelled by the collapse of Bradley Gibson to list for his personal recollection the collapses which had taken place in recent weeks.

4.6.5   We heard from many of our witnesses, and we agree, that the correct course of action would have been to call a case conference of all disciplines to consider each case individually and then to apply every mind available to thinking of a connection, the identification of which would bring the series to a halt. There were some consistent factors among the various collapses which might have come to light at such a conference, not least the fact that the alarm was raised each time by Beverly Allitt.

50

4.6.6   No such decisive and commanding action was forthcoming. It is impossible to say now whether a conference of this kind would have been effective in saving further lives or suffering. But it might have done and it should have been attempted.

4.7   Henry Chan

4.7.1   The day after Bradley Gibson collapsed, Yik Hung 'Henry' Chan suffered two severe episodes. The tentative conclusion that he had suffered convulsions secondary either to his head injury or to his high temperature seems reasonable. A chest x-ray taken in Nottingham the day after he was transferred showed that there was fluid on Henry's lungs. It has been argued that this was an indication that he had been suffocated, but there are a number of other possible explanations consistent with the diagnosis of convulsions or with the chest infection which he developed during the night when he was transferred.

4.7.2   However, there was still some uncertainty about the diagnosis of convulsions. Although convulsions can take the course described in the first episode, it is interesting that the experienced nurses who attended Henry did not believe that what they had seen was a typical febrile convulsion. Given that Henry was the third child in less than a week to be transferred to the Paediatric Intensive Care Unit at Queen's Medical Centre after collapsing unexpectedly, our conclusion in paragraph 4.6.5 is reinforced. Yet still no firm or vigorous action was taken.

4.7.3   On 4th April 1991, the Night Services Manager Mrs Jean Savill wrote a letter to Mrs Onions, the nurse manager responsible for Ward Four, expressing concern about staffing and equipment on Ward Four at night. We discuss the staffing levels on Ward Four, which Mrs Savill had raised several times in the preceding months, in section 5.8 and in section 5.11 we explore her concerns about resuscitation equipment. Her letter also stated that there had been two "cardiac arrests" on Ward Four in the last week and seven "cardiac arrests" during the last three months. It was copied to Dr Porter, Dr Nanayakkara, the Unit General Manager, Mr Martin Gibson, and to her own manager Mr Peter Flood. Mr Flood was the Assistant General Manager responsible for Patient Services, excluding Maternity, Gynaecology and Children's Services, which were managed by Miss Hannah Newton.

4.7.4   The purpose of this letter was to demonstrate the need for additional staffing at night on Ward Four, not to raise any question about the cause of the "cardiac arrests" to which it referred. Nevertheless, it was true that the 'crash team' had already been called to Ward Four seven times in 1991, including five times during March. In the previous three years, there had been no "cardiac arrest" calls for Ward Four. Dr Nanayakkara responded to Mrs Savill's letter by writing a letter of his own to Mrs Onions on 9th April. He stated his own view that only one child had a genuine "cardiac arrest", but acknowledged that there had been "quite a significant number of children having had emergency resuscitation offered". He said he would bring together information on all these children, but his purpose was to review the care that was given, not to look for a common cause.

4.7.5   The other recipients of Mrs Savill's letter realised that there had been a lot of very sick children on Ward Four in recent months, but they do not appear to have been alarmed by the number of "cardiac arrests" she referred to. Perhaps they were reassured by Dr Nanayakkara's letter, which was copied to the same people. Mr Gibson met Mrs Savill on 12th April to discuss her concerns about staffing and equipment. He did not get the impression that she thought the spate of collapses was suspicious or that it would continue.

4.8 Becky Phillips

4.8.1   On 5th April Becky Phillips died. We must bear in mind that she did not die on Ward Four. She died at home and was believed to be a victim of Sudden Infant Death Syndrome (SIDS), or 'cot death'. It is therefore unreasonable to suggest, as some accounts of the events on Ward Four have, that the staff should have reacted on the basis that there had been three deaths on the ward in six weeks. This was not so. There was far less reason to look for a link between Becky's death and the deaths of Liam Taylor and Timothy Hardwick than there was to look for a link with the three other cot deaths in the neighbourhood of Grantham which occurred at about this time.

4.8.2   On the other hand, Becky had been treated on Ward Four regularly since her birth and was well known by the staff. Many of them saw her looking well the day before she died, and they all heard about her death. While Becky's death is in one sense set aside from the series, it must have added to the growing concern on the ward.

4.8.3   We must also question how reasonable it was to conclude that Becky's death was a cot death just because no medical explanation could be found. The history of her last hours of life which her parents told to the doctors clearly showed that she had been in distress. But the General Practitioner who attended her was experienced and respected, and he believed that her symptoms that evening were of colic. Since nothing which might have caused Becky's death was found at the post mortem examination, the explanation offered was accepted. However, a witness has pointed out that, as its name implies, SIDS occurs suddenly and the symptoms preceding death might have cast doubt on this diagnosis.

4.8.4   The blood sample which was taken when Becky was brought to the Accident and Emergency Department at GKGH was later tested for insulin after suspicion about criminal administration had been raised by the case of Paul Crampton. It was found to contain 72,440 pmol/L of insulin, and less than 75 pmol/L of c-peptide. There was some dispute about the interpretation of these results at Allitt's trial, but they are consistent with the finding that the cause of Becky Phillips' death was that she, like Paul Crampton, had been injected with insulin[2].

4.8.5   Knowing this result, we might ask why the sample of Becky's blood was not tested for insulin sooner. The answer is that there was no reason to suspect that there would be a high concentration of insulin in Becky's blood. Very little is known about the effects of insulin overdose on babies, and Becky did not exhibit the symptoms expected in adults or older children. Other tests, including insulin assay, might have been carried out at the time if the diagnosis of SIDS had been questioned, but it was not.

4.8.6   We bear in mind that at this stage there was no suspicion that Paul Crampton had been injected with insulin, so there were no grounds for suspecting that this was the cause of Becky Phillips' death. The sample was taken for further testing at a later stage to help throw light on the causes of SIDS. It might never have been taken were it not for Dr Nanayakkara's interest in that syndrome, and it might never have been tested for insulin if Allitt had not used the same method to attack other children.

4.9 Katie Phillips

4.9.1   The next child to collapse unexpectedly was Katie Phillips, brought to Ward Four on 5th April for observation after her twin sister died. We have already mentioned that later in 1991 the police asked the Consultant Paediatric Radiologist at

---

[2]The relationship between insulin and c-peptide and its implications are explained in paragraph 4.5.3 above.

Queen's Medical Centre, Dr Phillip Small, to review all x-rays relating to the children whose cases they were investigating. When he examined the chest x-rays of Katie Phillips taken on 5th April 1991 at GKGH he observed rib fractures which appeared to be fresh. He also observed these fractures healing on x-rays taken on 18th April 1991 and 22nd May 1991. Two other experts examined the films before the trial of Beverly Allitt, one for the prosecution and the other for the defence. Both confirmed that healing fractures were clearly visible on 22nd May, but they stated that no definite fractures were visible on the earlier films.

4.9.2   The x-ray film taken on 5th April at GKGH was taken to Nottingham with Katie when she was transferred on 7th April. It was sent to the Radiology Department at GKGH when Katie was transferred back to Grantham and a written report was sent to Ward Four on 19th April. The x-ray taken on 18th April was reported by a radiologist on 23rd April. No rib fractures were reported on either film.

4.9.3   It is probable that the fractures were caused by shaking or squeezing, but they might also have been the result of vigorous cardiac massage. If the fractures had been observed at the time on the film taken on 5th April, before Katie had received cardiac massage, they might have raised suspicion that she had been deliberately harmed. Since it remains in dispute whether any fractures are visible on that film or on the film dated 18th April, we find no grounds for criticism of the GKGH radiologist, inasmuch as the rib fractures were obviously extremely difficult to detect.

4.9.4   Several other films were taken at GKGH on 7th April while Katie was receiving emergency treatment. These x-rays were reviewed on the ward and no fractures were observed, but there is no record of them being reviewed by a radiologist, either in Grantham or in Nottingham. The police were unable to trace these films. We were unable to discover when or how they disappeared.

We do not know whether a radiologist might have been able to detect rib fractures on these films more easily than on the film taken on 5th April. Their loss removed another potential piece of evidence of foul play. It demonstrates once more a lack of careful attention to detail.

4.9.5   Dr Small also detected the fractures on further x-rays, taken on 9th April at Nottingham City Hospital, presented to him at Allitt's trial. These x-rays were reviewed in the Radiology Department at the City Hospital and no rib fractures were observed.

4.9.6   Regardless of the additional evidence which may or may not have been present on the x-ray films, Katie's sudden illness was clearly unexpected and unexplained. On 20th April Dr Nanayakkara wrote to Dr Curnock, a Consultant Paediatrician at City Hospital who had been monitoring Katie's progress because of her low birth weight. In that letter, Dr Nanayakkara said, "When Katie was transferred ... it was suggested that Katie's behaviour and clinical condition may well have been a psychological reaction to Becky's sudden death. This is perhaps the only way I can explain the very traumatic and stormy course of events Katie went through following Becky's death". Clearly he had no idea why it had happened.

4.9.7   Katie Phillips was the fifth child to be transferred to Nottingham as an emergency in less than a month. Since Liam Taylor died at the end of February, five other children had stopped breathing unexpectedly while they were on Ward Four. In addition, Paul Crampton had suffered three, as yet unexplained, episodes of hypoglycaemia on the ward and Becky Phillips had died at home during the night after she was discharged.

4.9.8   We must continue to bear in mind that there were many other children on Ward Four during this period and to guard against the impression that the atmosphere on the ward was one of perpetual crisis revolving around the children whom Allitt had

56

attacked. On the basis of the information available at the time, there were good grounds for believing that at least two of the children whose cases we have described had suffered no more than an unexpected deterioration in the condition for which they had been admitted. But the staff on Ward Four were beginning to become worried by the sheer number of times the 'crash team' was being called to deal with emergencies on the ward. Hitherto this had been a rare occurrence, but it was becoming common.

4.9.9   The nurses and doctors on the ward began to discuss informally among themselves what might be causing babies and children on the ward to become so ill. We discuss the communication on the ward, both formal and informal, in section 5.10. Several people have told us that the possibility that some infection on the ward might be the cause was discussed, but we have found no evidence that any steps were taken to investigate this possibility, for example by having the ward screened for infection.

4.9.10   One of our expert witnesses, chosen and recommended to us by the Royal College of Physicians of London and himself a Consultant Paediatrician in charge of a Paediatric Unit in a District General Hospital, examined the patient records and some other documents at our invitation. After the most careful consideration, and warning himself against the dangers of retrospection, he told us that if such a series of episodes had occurred on his unit he would have closed it by 7th April and called a multi-disciplinary conference to seek a common cause. Such a course would also reassure himself and his subordinates that they were not at fault in some way in their management of the cases.

4.9.11   Closure of a children's ward is a serious matter and has many repercussions in terms of management, hospital morale and public confidence. These repercussions would be particularly serious in Grantham, because the nearest alternative service for children is over twenty miles away. In the absence of an identified infection requiring eradication or recognition of the epidemic nature of the episodes, we are not convinced that closure of the ward would have been the right course to follow. Neither would that step necessarily have been effective in the absence of any energetic action to resolve the problem. As matters stood, those responsible had not appreciated the nature of the problem and the question of closure had not arisen.

4.10 Michael Davidson

4.10.1   Beverly Allitt's next victim was Michael Davidson. Although his collapse was unexpected, it was accepted at the time by the surgeons and anaesthetists in charge of his case and by Dr Nanayakkara as due to an attack of overbreathing associated with carpopedal spasm. It was believed that this was brought about by Michael's anxiety about the injection. There did not seem to be any cause for suspicion until some time after the police investigation had begun. We must therefore note that he might reasonably not have been counted in the growing list of unexplained collapses.

4.10.2   On the other hand, the Junior House Surgeon who was giving the injection when Michael suddenly collapsed told us that what she observed was not, in her judgment, carpopedal spasm. Given the occurrence of a dramatic clinical event in the course of her injection, it is unfortunate that the possibility of a causal association was not considered and the remaining half of the contents of the syringe retained for analysis. Had this been done, contamination with a substance other than the antibiotic intended for Michael might have been detected. The failure to do so was in contravention of the South Lincolnshire Health Authority Policy for the Care and Custody of Drugs. However, it is perhaps understandable that the Junior House Surgeon, who was an inexperienced, newly qualified doctor, disposed of the syringe before she had recovered from the shock of Michael's collapse. She told us that there were present within a short time a

Consultant and SHO who were satisfied that the collapse had resulted from Michael's anxiety about having an injection, not from the substance being injected. It is nevertheless a fact that another possible piece of evidence was lost.

4.11 The 12th April 1991

4.11.1   On this crucial date, Dr Porter received a telephone call from the laboratory in Cardiff with the results of the tests on Paul Crampton's blood. Although the results showed that the blood contained a large quantity of exogenous insulin, Dr Porter had a number of uncertainties about the significance of this finding. He told us that he was even doubtful that the results related to Paul Crampton. He said he thought the sample of Paul's blood might have been mixed up with another sample, because the person who rang from Cardiff told him that he had not realised before their conversation that Paul was a child, nor that he was not diabetic. We have interviewed this person, who was the Chief Medical Laboratory Scientific Officer (MLSO). He told us that he was fully aware of these facts.

4.11.2   Assuming that the tests had been done on the correct sample, Dr Porter remained uncertain. He told us that he was not sure that a high insulin level with low c-peptide meant that the insulin was inevitably exogenous. He was not even certain that the c-peptide level reported was low for a child of Paul's age. The Cardiff laboratory, which has the special status of a Supra-regional Assay Service Laboratory, had in fact taken all possible steps to check the validity of their findings. There was insufficient blood for a complete re-run of the assay, but all the procedures involved, the calculations and the calibration of the instrumentation, had been re-checked in order to verify the result.

4.11.3   Despite his doubts, Dr Porter was nevertheless concerned that Paul Crampton might have been given exogenous insulin. He tried to contact Dr Derek Johnston at Queen's Medical Centre (QMC) but was unable to do so. He therefore spoke on the telephone to the Paediatric Registrar on call. The response he received from QMC is discussed in section 5.13.

4.11.4   Dr Porter told us that on the evening of Friday 12th April he also passed on the results from Cardiff to a junior doctor and, in the absence of the Ward Manager Sister Barker who had just departed for a week's annual leave, to a senior nurse. He said he told them to watch for any irregular activity but not to raise the alarm generally. When we interviewed the junior doctor in question, he denied knowledge of the insulin result until after the police were called. The Senior Staff Nurse concerned clearly recalled Dr Porter telling her about it on the ward, but she was not on duty from Friday 12th April to Tuesday 16th April inclusive. Dr Porter was away at the annual conference of the British Paediatric Association on Tuesday and Wednesday, 16th and 17th April, so it is hard to see how he could have told her before Thursday 18th April. It is difficult to establish clearly what went on, but whatever it was, it hardly constitutes decisive action to protect the children on the ward.

4.11.5   We acknowledge that it is difficult to imagine that someone in a hospital has attempted to murder a child patient. In view of his doubts referred to above, Dr Porter checked other possible explanations of the result he had received before taking action. But we would expect this to have been done as a matter of great urgency, and the police to have been informed as soon as other explanations had been excluded. In fact, it was more than two weeks before the police were called. In that time, four further children were attacked, including Claire Peck who died.

4.11.6   We were not able to establish clearly when and in what terms Dr Porter informed Mrs Onions, the nurse manager responsible for Ward Four, of the Cardiff results. It appears that he told her either on Friday evening, 12th April, or on Monday 15th April. Mrs Onions told us that he did not mention any specific result, but just told her he thought Paul Crampton might have been given exogenous insulin.

4.11.7 Dr Porter and Mrs Onions discussed the possibility that Paul Crampton might have been given accidentally the dose of insulin intended for a diabetic child on the ward. We were told in evidence that such a large accidental dosage is highly unlikely. Nevertheless Mrs Onions was told to check the notes of any diabetic children who might have been on the ward around the same period, to see whether this was possible. Mrs Onions also said she would ask the unit pharmacist to check whether more insulin than usual had been supplied to Ward Four, which she did the same day and was told that there had been no increase. In the meantime Dr Porter would investigate his doubts about the significance of the results in the medical library.

4.11.8 It was probably after this conversation with Mrs Onions, and certainly on Monday 15th April, that Dr Porter told Dr Nanayakkara about the result. Again, the way in which the result was conveyed by Dr Porter appears to have communicated more of his uncertainty as to its significance than of the implications if it was accurate. Dr Nanayakkara accepted that Dr Porter intended to establish the explanation for the results and apparently thought no more of it for the rest of the week. His own concerns to discover what had caused the unexpected and unexplained collapses on the ward prompted him to try to obtain all the medical notes of the children concerned to conduct a full medical audit. This initiative seems not to have been completed, for reasons we explain in paragraph 4.16.10.

4.11.9 Although it is difficult to determine precisely at this distance when the checks agreed by Dr Porter and Mrs Onions were carried out, it appears that all of them took days rather than the minutes one might expect. We return to the outcome of these checks and the action which followed in section 4.14. It is with regret that we see these steps as feeble and indecisive while Allitt continued on her deadly course.

4.12 Christopher Peasgood

4.12.1   It was the day after Dr Porter received the call from Cardiff that baby Christopher Peasgood stopped breathing suddenly on two occasions and was transferred to Nottingham. Although he was suffering from bronchiolitis, his collapses at that point were unexpected. The possible explanations were not supported by tests carried out in Nottingham, but there was no unequivocal evidence that he had been attacked.

4.13 Christopher King

4.13.1   On Tuesday, 16th April, Dr Porter left Grantham to attend the annual conference of the British Paediatric Association (BPA). Just as he left, Christopher King, who had undergone an operation for pyloric stenosis the previous evening, went blue and stopped breathing. The locum standing in for Dr Porter, who had only just arrived, was immediately called to Christopher, but he could not be expected to notice the similarities of Christopher King's symptoms to those of Christopher Peasgood, whom he had not seen. Dr Porter knew both of his collapse and of all that had gone before. He went so far as to advise his colleague before he left to check Christopher's blood sugar.

4.14 Wednesday and Thursday, 17th and 18th April

4.14.1   Dr Porter returned to Grantham on the evening of Wednesday, 17th April, allowing Dr Nanayakkara to attend the conference on Thursday and Friday. It has seemed odd to us that these two Consultants should have left their unit to attend a conference when what can only be described as a mounting crisis remained unresolved. But of course the real problem is that they had not fully recognised the magnitude of the crisis; if they had done, and had planned decisive action, they probably would have stayed to see it executed.

4.14.2   While he was at the BPA conference, Dr Porter heard a presentation about Munchausen Syndrome by Proxy. This syndrome is discussed further in section 5.4, but for now we should stress that the presentation referred to cases of parents inducing or fabricating illness or injury in their own children. Dr Porter was impressed by the use of video recording equipment to detect these cases, and wondered whether it might be used to see whether someone was indeed attacking children on Ward Four.

4.14.3   Meanwhile, Mrs Onions had obtained from the Medical Records Department the records of Paul Crampton and of the two diabetic children who had been on Ward Four at about the same time as he. She checked their dates of admission and discharge and found that neither of them was on the ward when Paul was there. It was therefore impossible that insulin intended for one of them might have been given to Paul accidentally. However, for some reason Mrs Onions did not feel that she could completely rule out this possibility without going through the prescription charts with Sister Barker, who was due to return from her holiday the following Monday.

4.14.4   Mrs Onions told us that she informed Dr Porter some time before Friday 19th April that she had established as firmly as she could for the time being that Paul Crampton had not been given insulin accidentally. Dr Porter confirmed that he knew by Friday evening. Since Dr Porter did not return to Grantham until Wednesday 17th April, it seems probable that he received the information from Mrs Onions on Thursday 18th April.

4.15 Patrick Elstone

4.15.1   Thursday 18th April was also the day when Patrick Elstone's two collapses occurred. Dr Porter attended the first, when Patrick had been found grey and with shallow breathing. Patrick's parents were not informed of this collapse. They did not have a telephone in their home and there was no answer at the number they had given to the nurses. Since Patrick had recovered quickly, it was decided not to ask the police to visit them, which was the alternative means of contacting them.

4.15.2   We can understand why this judgment was made and do not wish to criticise the nurse responsible. Nevertheless it is an unfortunate fact that, if Patrick's parents had known, they would have gone to the hospital and stayed with him and the second, more serious attack might have been prevented. Mrs Elstone told us that she had found a bruise on Patrick's forehead earlier the same day.   She informed the nursing staff, but it was not investigated or recorded in the notes. This was a lapse from proper procedures.

4.15.3   When Patrick Elstone collapsed a second time, at 8.00pm, it was the Locum Consultant, who had stayed on to stand in for Dr Nanayakkara when Dr Porter returned, who was called to see him.   This was the second child he had seen blue and struggling for breath on Ward Four during the four days he had been there. He told us that this did not surprise him. He believed that both children's collapses could be explained by their existing illness. He was not aware of the background of other collapses and deaths on the ward. The next day he informed Dr Porter of what had happened and left Grantham when Dr Nanayakkara returned from the BPA conference later in the day.

4.16 Friday to Monday, 19th to 22nd April

4.16.1   Mrs Onions told us that she and Dr Porter arranged to meet on Friday 19th April to discuss the outcome of her review of the notes of diabetic patients to determine whether Paul Crampton might have been injected with insulin accidentally. She told us that Dr Porter was busy all day and that the meeting did not take place.   Dr Porter told us he was unaware of this arrangement.

4.16.2   By this stage Dr Porter had overcome his other doubts about the interpretation of the results of the tests on Paul's blood. Having heard about Christopher King and Patrick Elstone from the locum, he was very worried.   When Dr Nanayakkara telephoned in the evening of Friday 19th April to say he had returned from the BPA conference, Dr Porter told him of his concerns and the action he proposed to take.

4.16.3   That evening, Dr Porter telephoned Mrs Onions at home and asked her to arrange for the installation of video surveillance on the ward.   She told him she did not have authority to do this, but she agreed to ensure that the side door to the ward was locked so that no-one could enter the ward without passing the nurses' station.

4.16.4   Dr Porter also made a number of other telephone calls that evening.   First, he telephoned the Paediatric Senior Registrar on call at Queen's Medical Centre to suggest that they measure the level of insulin in Patrick Elstone's blood.

4.16.5   Dr Porter's next step was to try to contact Mr Martin Gibson, the Unit General Manager, but he was not at home. On hearing that Dr Porter had rung, Mr Gibson telephoned Mr Stuart Jackson, the duty manager for that weekend, and asked him to ring Dr Porter. This was because, according to Mr Gibson, Dr Porter had acquired a reputation for what Mr Gibson described as "fanciful ideas", by which we understood him to mean a tendency to raise alarms which were not justified in the event. Mr Gibson was trying to encourage Dr Porter to use the duty manager system set up to handle problems which arose at weekends.   Dr Porter explained his concerns to Mr Jackson and repeated his request for video surveillance on the ward.   Mr Jackson said this would be difficult to arrange.   He said he would talk to Mr Gibson.

4.16.6   Although both Consultants told us that they had discussed the matter on Friday evening, they had not come to a definite conclusion that insulin had been administered to Paul

Crampton deliberately. Mrs Onions and Mr Jackson both took the view that no drastic action should be taken unless the two Consultants could agree that this was what the clinical evidence showed. They told us that they made this clear to Dr Porter.

4.16.7   On Saturday 20th April Mr Jackson telephoned Mrs Onions to discuss with her what Dr Porter had said. He told her that Mr Gibson was not inclined to take any action unless she and Dr Nanayakkara discussed the matter with Dr Porter and came to a common view. For her own part, Mrs Onions alleges that she was unaware that Dr Porter had a specific result to back up his suspicions and she was not convinced that there was anything criminal going on.

4.16.8   The weekend passed with no further incidents on the ward. Dr Porter was becoming increasingly worried, but he did not feel able to call the police himself. On Sunday evening, he sat down to draw up a list of similarities between the various children whose conditions had deteriorated unexpectedly on Ward Four and a plan of action if anything similar should happen again.

4.16.9   On Monday 22nd April Mrs Onions passed on to her manager, Miss Hannah Newton, what Dr Porter had said. We find it surprising that Mrs Onions did not think it necessary to pass on such dramatic information to her manager immediately. Like Mr Gibson, Miss Newton wanted to be sure that other explanations had been ruled out before taking the action Dr Porter had requested. She described Dr Porter as "a bit unpredictable". She was clearly influenced by the fact that Mrs Onions did not believe that anyone could have injected Paul Crampton with insulin deliberately, and that Dr Nanayakkara apparently did not share Dr Porter's concern.

4.16.10   Later that day, Dr Nanayakkara, Dr Porter and Mrs Onions met to discuss matters related to the children who had collapsed. The three of them agreed that steps needed to be taken to establish precisely what was happening on the ward, but they did not reach any conclusion about the implications of the results of the tests on Paul Crampton's blood. Dr Nanayakkara said he would carry out an audit of the notes of the children involved. Mrs Onions reported to Miss Newton that this had been agreed. The audit was never completed, because the medical files of some of the children who had been transferred to Nottingham were still there.

4.16.11 Following the meeting, Dr Nanayakkara wrote a long letter to Mr Gibson, the burden of which was not, as might have been expected, that some undiscovered and sinister factor was causing children on Ward Four to collapse. It related principally to the needs in terms of equipment for the ward to respond to such collapses. Dr Nanayakkara mentioned that Paul Crampton's hypoglycaemia was "secondary to probable external administration of insulin", but he played down the possibility that someone was deliberately harming children on the ward. Dr Nanayakkara told us that he mentioned this possibility only because of Dr Porter's suspicions. At this stage, he himself did not believe that this was the explanation.

4.16.12 Although Dr Nanayakkara's letter did not present strongly the possibility that the events on Ward Four were the result of deliberate action, it did make clear that there had been a "most unusual and unexplained spate of emergencies" and that close consideration was needed to identify a common cause. For some reason this letter did not reach Mr Gibson until 30th April. Dr Nanayakkara also sent copies to Miss Newton, who received hers on Monday evening, 29th April, and to Mr Peter Flood, who received his copy on 30th April.

4.16.13 Sister Barker returned from her holiday on Monday 22nd April and came on duty at 1.00pm. The senior staff nurse whom Dr Porter had told about Paul Crampton's blood analysis told Sister Barker what he had said about it, but it was not until after Claire Peck died that evening that Dr Porter himself mentioned it. He asked Sister Barker to keep Claire's infusion fluids for testing. When she asked him why, he told her about his fear that someone had been harming children deliberately and they went on to discuss the results of the insulin assay on Paul Crampton's blood.

4.17 Claire Peck

4.17.1   Later on Monday, 22nd April, Claire Peck died. Even after her death, it was more than a week before the police were called to Ward Four. Claire's death certificate recorded that she died from "status asthmaticus", an asthma attack which was not responding to treatment. She was indeed very ill with her asthma attack, but her sudden collapse and failure to respond to resuscitation were highly unusual. It is very rare for children to die from asthma in hospital.

4.17.2   There were two pieces of evidence at the time to suggest that Claire's death was suspicious and to link it to the previous cases. First, once her heart had stopped, it was unusually difficult to restart it. This had also been observed in the cases of Liam Taylor, Bradley Gibson and Katie Phillips, and is now believed to indicate that she had been given some drug which affected her heart.

4.17.3   The second piece of evidence was that blood samples, taken while efforts were continuing to resuscitate Claire and after her death, showed that the concentration of potassium in her blood was greater than 10 mmol/l. We have already explained the effects of potassium on the heart. There was broad agreement among those who were asked to give evidence on behalf of the prosecution and defence at Beverly Allitt's trial that if potassium had been injected intravenously in a dose large enough to give such a high concentration as was measured, it could be expected to have caused Claire's heart to stop.

4.17.4   However, the first sample in which the potassium was measured was taken 45 minutes after Claire's heart had stopped. The resuscitation team succeeded in restoring a normal heart rhythm for a few seconds shortly before the sample was taken, but for the rest of the intervening period her heart was either stopped or beating erratically.   The high concentration of potassium measured may have been due in part to the effects of prolonged cardiac arrest and acidosis on the concentration of potassium in the blood, discussed in paragraph 4.6.2 above, and may also have been because the blood sample had become 'haemolysed'.   Haemolysis is the term applied to the rupturing of red blood cells.   As a result of it, potassium leaks out into the non-cellular compartment of the blood where it is measured. It was not certain that the sample had not been 'haemolysed'.

4.17.5   It has also been suggested that Allitt might have killed Claire by injecting her with an overdose of lignocaine, an anaesthetic drug which in large doses can cause epileptic fits and stop the heart.   In February 1993, tests on the sample of Claire's blood taken after her death showed that it did contain a small amount of lignocaine.   The amount measured was consistent with Claire having been given a massive dose before she collapsed, since her body would have continued to clear the lignocaine until she died.

4.17.6   The measurement of lignocaine might therefore have given another clue that Claire had been murdered.   On the other hand, lignocaine is sometimes used to correct abnormal rhythms of the heart and the amount measured is also consistent with a therapeutic dose having been given as part of the resuscitation attempt. Although the doctors involved did not believe that they had used lignocaine to treat Claire, it cannot be excluded as a possibility.   We doubt if this result in itself would have led to suspicion if lignocaine had been measured at the time.   In fact, there was no reason to test for lignocaine.

4.17.7   Bearing in mind that it was not suggested until nearly two years later that Claire Peck might have been given lignocaine, it is not reasonable to expect Dr Porter to have thought of it. Extensive investigations of the cause of Claire's death were indeed put in hand by Dr Porter, but the post mortem examination was conducted before the results were available and the post mortem report accepted that her death was due to natural causes. It is fortunate that no further children were attacked in the last week before the police were called.

4.18 Tuesday 23rd April to Tuesday 30th April

4.18.1   On Tuesday, 23rd April, Mrs Onions asked Sister Barker to complete her check on the medical files to make sure that insulin intended for a diabetic child on the ward could not have been given to Paul Crampton accidentally. Sister Barker told us that she never believed that this was likely, but she checked the files as requested. When we interviewed Sister Barker, she was sure that she told Mrs Onions that she had ruled out the possibility of accidental administration before Mrs Onions went on holiday on Thursday, 25th April. Yet Miss Newton told us that when she spoke to Mrs Onions the day before she went on holiday, Mrs Onions told her that she had not yet been able to complete the check.

4.18.2   We accept that the possibility of accidental administration had to be eliminated, but it should have been done a great deal more quickly than it was. In fact, the half-hearted pursuit of this false trail contributed to Mrs Onions' and Miss Newton's inactivity with regard to the alternative explanation, which turned out to be the true one, that the insulin had been injected deliberately.

4.18.3   On Wednesday 24th April, the last day before her holiday, Mrs Onions wrote a letter to Miss Newton. The letter began, "As the staff morale is now at an all time low..." and went on to say that it was very difficult to provide a safe environment on the ward within the present staffing establishment. Like Dr Nanayakkara's letter of 23rd April, the main thrust of this letter concerned the need for additional resources on the ward. The letter mentioned "numerous cardiac and respiratory emergencies", but gave no indication of any suspicion as to the cause of these emergencies.

4.18.4   Mrs Onions' letter may have lacked sufficient detail, but it clearly reads as a cry for help from someone faced with a crisis situation. Miss Newton's reply, dated 13th May 1991, can only be described as a cold rebuff. The letter criticises Mrs Onions for not providing a more detailed analysis and producing solutions herself and goes on to outline the information needed to back up the case for additional staff. We acknowledge that this must be seen against the background of communication between these two managers regarding the staffing situation. The staffing of Ward Four is discussed in section 5.8. Nevertheless, we would expect Miss Newton to have taken more urgent and sympathetic action in response to Mrs Onions' letter, particularly in view of the series of disasters of which she was well aware.

4.18.5   From this time until Monday 29th April, it appears that everyone involved was waiting for someone else to do something. Mr Gibson was still waiting to hear the outcome of the meeting between the two Consultants and Mrs Onions. Miss Newton was waiting to hear whether the results from Cardiff must mean that Paul Crampton had been given insulin deliberately. Dr Porter and Dr Nanayakkara believed that they had given sufficient information to Mrs Onions and Mr Gibson and that it was for them to decide what action was appropriate to prevent a recurrence. Mrs Onions was on holiday.

4.18.6   On Monday 29th April, Dr Porter received a telephone call from Professor Sir David Hull at Queen's Medical Centre. The circumstances which prompted Sir David to make this call are discussed in section 5.13. Sir David urged Dr Porter to go direct to senior management and ask them to call the police. Dr Porter went to see Mr Gibson. They had only a brief conversation as Mr Gibson was on the way to a meeting, but Mr Gibson said he would telephone the police the next day.

4.18.7   Meanwhile, Miss Newton was making her weekly visit to Ward Four. Sister Barker told her that neither of the diabetic children was on the ward at the same time as Paul Crampton. That afternoon, there was a fire in one of the cubicles on the ward. The fire brigade were unable to find any match or cigarette end which might have started the fire accidentally. Following the fire, Miss Newton met Dr Porter, who had just returned from seeing Mr Gibson. Dr Porter told her about his conversation with Professor Sir David Hull and said that he was now sure of the significance of the results.

4.18.8   Both Miss Newton and Mr Gibson had one remaining doubt: whether Dr Nanayakkara shared Dr Porter's concern. This was no reason for delay. This doubt was removed when they received their copies of Dr Nanayakkara's letter dated 23rd April. Miss Newton received her copy when she returned to her office after meeting Dr Porter; Mr Gibson received his on Tuesday morning. We have been unable to discover why it took this letter nearly a week to travel a short distance across the hospital.

4.18.9   Mr Gibson telephoned the police during the morning of Tuesday 30th April, after receiving his copy of Dr Nanayakkara's letter. Miss Newton had tried to contact him first thing, but he had been unavailable. He rang her back mid-morning to tell her that he had arranged a meeting with the police that afternoon. When Sir David Hull rang Dr Porter later that day to find out what had been done in response to his earlier call, Dr Porter told him that the police had been called.

4.19 Conclusion

4.19.1　　Reviewing the events described in this chapter, it is clear that there were several possible clues to the hidden cause of the sudden collapses on Ward Four.　The extent to which we have been critical of the failure to detect or pick up these clues has varied in accordance with their potential for identifying the true cause of the collapses.　But we can only speculate as to what might have happened if any or all of these failures had not occurred.

4.19.2　　The first clear evidence of foul play emerged on Friday 12th April: the results which showed that Paul Crampton had been injected with exogenous insulin.　We feel bound to record that in our judgment the delays between receipt of these results from Cardiff and the calling of the police, which ended Allitt's criminal course, cannot be justified.　More prompt action might well have saved the life of Claire Peck and the sufferings of three other children.

4.19.3　　We find difficulty in apportioning the blame for what happened as between the individuals mentioned.　The true cause of the cumulative failures to act upon information which was there to be seen was a general lack of the qualities of leadership, energy and drive in all those most closely connected with the management of Ward Four.

4.19.4　　There was certainly no evidence of lack of clinical skill and conscientious care on the part of the Consultants.　The fact that more of the children did not suffer death or permanent injury can largely be attributed to their skill and persistence. Their failure was not to grasp with energy the problem presented by the highly unusual events that they were witnessing and to take systematic and decisive steps to elucidate their cause.

4.19.5　　On the management side, the failure was in lack of leadership and effective communication in a structure with no clear definitions of responsibility or accountability. Although a highly efficient and well-regulated organisation might still be vulnerable at the hands of a person like Allitt, the weaknesses that we have identified at nearly all levels of the GKGH administration provided poor protection against the unexpected.

4.19.6   It is not possible to predict every kind of criminal behaviour and guard against it, particularly when that behaviour is unprecedented as it was in this case, at least in the United Kingdom.   However, the Grantham experience demonstrates the danger of assuming that there must be a natural explanation even where one cannot be found.   We now know that child abuse and murder can be and have been perpetrated in hospital.   However unlikely it may seem at the time, we conclude that when faced with a clinical history in a child that defies rational explanation, constant awareness of the possibility of unnatural events is essential.

CHAPTER FIVE: GENERAL THEMES

5.1 Introduction

5.1.1   In this chapter we return to consider a number of matters which are peripheral to the disaster, but which may have some bearing on the course of events.

5.2 Attacks on Hospital Patients

5.2.1   It may be thought that previous acquaintance with or experience of attacks on patients might have prompted earlier detection of Beverly Allitt. We set aside the vengeful attack on a patient by an intruder which undoubtedly occurs. But attacks in hospital on patients by nurses and on children by their mothers, though rare, are not unheard of. Only such unnatural crimes as these need be considered in our context. The causes of these attacks must be rooted in some form of mental instability and in this case the cause has been loosely associated with the illness called Munchausen Syndrome, which we must now consider.

5.3 Munchausen syndrome

5.3.1   The term Munchausen Syndrome was introduced in 1951 by a physician of erudition and wit to describe a particular form of hospital addiction. The fictional character, Baron von Munchausen, travelled widely and told stories of exploits that were beyond credibility. Those with whom his name is now associated travel from hospital to hospital with stories of medical disorder, often severe and dramatic, and usually supported by pathological evidence. The latter may be falsified, such as by the artificial contamination of urine with blood or by self-injury, such as the application of a tight ligature, or it may be a result of previous disease or injury. Admission to hospital is often achieved and one of the most remarkable aspects of the disorder is the extent to which those afflicted subject themselves to investigation, often involving prolonged and painful procedures and often culminating in exploratory operation.

5.3.2   The attachment of the Munchausen label is, and should be, restricted to those with florid and bizarre disorders of the types described above. Fictitious complaints and self-inflicted injuries are encountered relatively frequently and need not represent the serious disorder of behaviour that characterises those with Munchausen Syndrome.

5.3.3   Beverly Allitt had a history of frequent minor injuries which were eventually recognised as having been self-inflicted. She also had abdominal and urinary complaints for which she was investigated. In October 1990 her appendix was removed, but was found to be normal. The wound became infected twice in the weeks following operation raising, in retrospect, the possibility that she interfered with it. In spite of the nature and frequency of her various disorders, which might in themselves have raised doubts about her suitability for the nursing profession, there were insufficient grounds at the time she was recruited for making a formal diagnosis of Munchausen Syndrome in the terms in which it has come to be used. We have already referred (paragraphs 2.2.5 and 2.3.4) to evidence we have heard that it is not uncommon for young people to enjoy the attention which injury attracts.

5.3.4   In the Summer of 1991, by which time Allitt was on bail following her arrest, her medical history became more florid and bizarre. In July 1991, when she was in hospital in Peterborough, the diagnosis of Munchausen Syndrome was first suggested. Confirmation of factitious interference was provided by her manipulation of thermometer readings to temperatures that were totally incompatible with her clinical state. Furthermore, at

76

the same time she was complaining of an enlarged right breast. No cause was found, but three small puncture marks in her breast were observed. These marks probably indicated that she had injected herself with water. In retrospect the diagnosis was irrefutable. However, no criticism can be levelled because the diagnosis was not made sooner. In our judgment there were insufficient grounds for suspecting the serious disorder of behaviour that characterises Munchausen Syndrome at the time that Allitt was recruited as an enrolled nurse to Ward Four.

5.4 Munchausen Syndrome by Proxy

5.4.1   This term, first introduced by Professor Roy Meadow in 1977, is applied to a situation in which factitious injury or manifestation of illness is inflicted on others. The victims, usually children, suffer in a way that is comparable to the self-inflicted suffering of those with Munchausen Syndrome. The frequent reports that Beverly Allitt suffered from Munchausen Syndrome by Proxy betray ignorance of the meaning of the term as defined by Professor Meadow and demonstrate the confusion which has been introduced into the understanding of what is essentially a form of child abuse. Occasionally this abuse can be directed against elderly or handicapped people who are equally vulnerable. About a quarter of the perpetrators of the abuse subsumed under the label of Munchausen Syndrome by Proxy themselves suffer from Munchausen Syndrome, but in general those with Munchausen Syndrome do not harm others.

5.4.2   In nearly all of the cases of Munchausen Syndrome by Proxy recorded in the literature, the abuse has been perpetrated by mothers on their own children, although there have been cases involving fathers, grandparents and other relatives or carers, but not nurses in a hospital setting. It has, however, been noted that 15-20% of the mothers involved have had some training in nursing.

5.4.3   Our searches have disclosed only two previous formal reports of nurses attacking their child patients. One occurred in Toronto, Canada and the other in Texas, USA. Neither case was reported in the British journals at the time, but both were reported in the New England Journal of Medicine in 1985.

5.4.4   The case in Toronto arose from a dramatic increase in the mortality rate in the cardiology ward of a children's hospital between July 1980 and March 1981. Although most of the children who died had serious congenital heart disease, their deaths often occurred at an unexpected time, and their clinical history was consistent with poisoning with digoxin. In four patients, forensic scientific and routine laboratory digoxin measurements suggested digoxin had been administered shortly before death.

5.4.5   A nurse was arrested and accused of administering these overdoses in March 1981. Charges against her were dismissed when further evidence showed that digoxin had been administered to another child while she was not on duty. An epidemiological investigation found that one nurse was on duty for all but two of the deaths, far more than the nurse who was originally accused. This second nurse was never arrested.

5.4.6   The second case occurred in the paediatric intensive care unit at a large medical centre in Texas, USA. Between April 1981 and June 1982 there was an unusual increase in the number of deaths and arrests in the unit. No cause for this increase could be found. It was noted that most of the incidents occurred during the evening work shift, and in the presence of one nurse. This nurse was never charged with murder in respect of these incidents, but she was charged and convicted in 1984 on one count of attempted murder. It remains unclear whether she caused the increase in the numbers of deaths.

5.4.7   Neither of the two cases described above is said to have involved someone with a previous history of Munchausen

Syndrome. The motivation for the alleged crimes is not discussed in the reports and the syndrome is not even mentioned.

5.4.8 Distinguished as is the New England Journal of Medicine, it is not, according to the evidence before us, required reading for the average practitioner in this country. Accordingly we cannot find that the doctors at GKGH were at fault for not being acquainted with the only two reported instances of nurses attacking children in their care. It should also be noted that in both these reported series, many months elapsed before the untoward events were recognised and stopped: seven months in the first series and fourteen in the second, making the point that lack of awareness of the unexpected may blind us to the reality.

5.4.9 Other articles of a journalistic character appeared in Nursing Times and Nursing Standard in 1986 and 1989 respectively, reporting previous instances of nurses being suspected of killing children in their care. But more commonly the crimes committed by nurses were against elderly patients. The only established instances of a nurse killing a child seem to have occurred outside this country. Statistically such an event was, and remains, a very remote possibility in the United Kingdom.

5.4.10 Against this background, we can find no grounds for believing that anyone was in a position to predict the danger in which Allitt's employment as a nurse would place her patients. We noted in section 5.3 that there was little reason to suspect that Allitt was suffering from Munchausen Syndrome before she was appointed to Ward Four. Nor do we find the term Munchausen Syndrome by Proxy helpful in the context of our Inquiry. As we have pointed out, there is a remarkable degree of confusion in the medical literature as to its precise meaning and as to whether it is the victim or the perpetrator that suffers from the syndrome. Furthermore, the application of an eponymous title runs the risk of implying unjustified certitude and of dignifying with a diagnostic label a horrific human deviance the origin and motivation of which are totally beyond the comprehension of normal people.

5.4.11   Whilst in this section we have stated that Allitt's progression from her erratic early medical history to that bizarre disorder that we classify as Munchausen Syndrome could not have been predicted, **we recommend** that no candidate for nursing in whom there is evidence of major personality disorder should be employed in the profession.

5.5 Role of Occupational Health

5.5.1   Beverly Allitt was screened in the Occupational Health (OH) Department at GKGH both when she was recruited to pupil nurse training, and when she was appointed to Ward Four. On both occasions she was passed fit for employment as a nurse. Prior to the second screening, she had been seen several times in the OH Department during the course of her training.

5.5.2   In considering the role of Occupational Health, we must ask ourselves whether the nurses and the doctor who saw Allitt might have expressed concern about her health to her managers. Given the frequency and nature of her ailments during her pre-nursing course and her pupil nurse training, there might have been a hint of caution about employing someone whose poor health was likely, if it continued, to make her an unreliable employee.

5.5.3   We remind the reader that Allitt's sickness record is relevant to our Inquiry only in so far as it might have provided a clue to her personality disorder and its disastrous consequences. We concern ourselves in this section with whether opportunities were available to the OH Department to recognise and draw attention to a suspicion of self-inflicted injury. We conclude the chapter by exploring how the OH service in the NHS might be improved so as to increase the chances of identifying people like Allitt. Our recommendations are expressed in terms of nursing because that is the profession which Allitt entered, but we recognise that the problems are not restricted to nursing. Our recommendations might usefully be applied to other professions which give access to patients.

5.5.4   OH physicians and nurses are concerned with the health of the employee with respect to their work. It is their task to ensure that an employee has a healthy and safe working environment, and is fit to do the job for which he or she is employed. The task begins with a pre-employment health screening. Its aim is to ensure that employing someone does not carry a risk of harm to self, to fellow employees or, in the case of the NHS, to patients.

5.5.5   Allitt was first seen by an OH nurse on the day of her interview for pupil nurse training. She was asked to complete a questionnaire about her health. The OH nurse had no information about her other than her answers to this document. As we noted in paragraph 2.4.2 above, no reference had been requested from Grantham College and she did not know how much time Allitt had missed through sickness during the second year of her pre-nursing course. She asked her a few questions, measured her height, weight and blood pressure and tested her vision, her colour vision and a urine sample. A chest x-ray showed no abnormalities. Finding no reason to doubt Allitt's health, the OH nurse passed her fit for employment.

5.5.6   During her pupil nurse training, Allitt was a regular attender at the Occupational Health Department. We have heard in evidence that many of the young pupil nurses living away from home for the first time attended OH regularly as a substitute for family support. The OH nurse got to know Allitt well and saw no reason to doubt her accounts of her illnesses. In retrospect, one might conclude that Allitt's regular attendances at OH were harbingers of more serious disorder, but at the time and individually they did not cause concern. The OH nurse did not receive a sickness referral from Allitt's tutors. She received reports of only a few of Allitt's attendances in the Accident and Emergency Department at GKGH. There was no reason for her to think that the minor ailments Allitt reported were causing any problems at work.

5.5.7   It is clear that there was here a failure of communication between the School of Nursing and Occupational Health during Allitt's training. Each side appears to have expected to hear from the other if a member of staff was not fit for work. Yet without information from the other, neither was in a position to make that judgment. We cannot know what conclusions they would have reached about Allitt had they discussed her. Neither had access to her hospital medical records or to those of her General Practitioner. It is a matter of speculation whether, had they discussed her, either side would have changed their view that her illnesses were genuine and her injuries accidental. It seems to us however that pooling their information might have stimulated further exploration of the underlying cause of her repeated complaints.

5.5.8   We noted in Chapter Two the shortcomings of the administrative arrangements surrounding Allitt's health screen when she was appointed as an enrolled nurse to Ward Four. The full-time OH nurse at GKGH had left in December 1990 and was not replaced until March 1991. Allitt was screened by an OH nurse from Pilgrim Hospital in Boston, one of a group who took it in turns to cover the work at GKGH during the gap.

5.5.9   This nurse did not know why the screening interview had been arranged. It had not been requested in writing. She understood mistakenly that Allitt had been in post on Ward Four since December 1990, and that she, the nurse, was being asked to confirm her fitness. In her evidence to us, she said she did not think that this misapprehension would have affected significantly the way she conducted the interview. But obviously she had in mind that Allitt had been on the ward for nearly three months, during which her manager had not mentioned any sickness problems.

5.5.10   The nurse questioned Allitt quite closely about her health.   Again, she had no independent source of information against which to verify what Allitt told her other than the brief notes which had been taken when she referred herself to OH. Allitt told her that she had missed about 80 days during her training through sickness.   This was considerably less than the true figure of 126 days, but enough to make the nurse refer her to the OH physician for his advice.

5.5.11   The doctor did not see Allitt himself at this stage. Having scrutinised the OH notes, he decided she was fit for employment. However, because of her history, he made a note to see her in April.   When he saw her on 9th April, Allitt had lost only one further day through sickness, so he saw no particular cause for concern.

5.5.12   Given their dependence on Allitt for information, it is hardly surprising that the OH Department did not suspect that she was in any way unfit for employment.

5.5.13   Many of those who have given evidence to us have pointed out that it is common for newly-qualified nurses to be treated as internal applicants when they apply for a post in the hospital where they undertook their practical training.   This can mean that they are not subjected to the usual pre-employment screening.   This was not so in Allitt's case and there was very little difference between the screening she underwent when she was appointed to Ward Four and her initial screening on entry to nurse training.   However, as a general rule we recommend that nurses should undergo formal health screening when they obtain their first posts after qualifying.   This represents the first opportunity to review the effect which the stress of nursing may be having on a nurse's mental and physical health.

5.5.14   Occupational Health departments would be in a better position to fulfil their role if they had better access to the information which is held by the hospital management and by schools of nursing in the case of learners. Every personnel department keeps records of employees' absence through sickness. **We recommend** that the possibility be reviewed of these records, and any other records of absence through sickness from any institution which the applicant has attended, being made available to OH departments. **We also recommend** that procedures for management referrals to OH should make clear the criteria which should trigger such referrals.

5.5.15   We have sought to discover if there is any way in which a serious personality disorder could be detected at a pre-employment screening interview. It has been suggested that some kind of psychological questionnaire might be used, but the evidence we have heard suggests that such questionnaires cannot be relied upon to detect personality disorder and furthermore they tend to be lengthy and to require interpretation by psychologists.

5.5.16   The Chairman of the Association of NHS Occupational Physicians (ANHOPS) advised us that it is very difficult to assess psychological health, and in particular to detect those with personality disorder. She suggested that excessive absence through sickness, excessive use of counselling or medical facilities, or self-harming behaviour such as attempted suicide, self-laceration or eating disorder are better guides than psychological testing. She suggested that applicants who show one or more of these patterns should not be accepted for training until they have shown the ability to live an independent life without professional support and have been in stable employment for at least two years.

5.5.17   We endorse this suggestion. It would allow those young people who are going through a temporary phase of attention-seeking behaviour during the maturing process to develop and stabilise. There is a risk that it would delay or even deter the entry of some who are ready for a career in nursing, and that it would be an unfair punishment for an unhappy period in their lives. However, we consider that this risk would be outweighed by the benefits. Not only might patients be protected from the minority among this group who might harm them, but the candidates themselves might be spared the stress of nursing until they were better able to cope with it. **We recommend** that further consideration be given to how this suggestion could be applied in practice.

5.5.18 Another suggestion has been that OH departments should have access to medical records of all candidates for employment. However, the requirements of medical confidentiality make this as a general rule quite impracticable. But that some occupations should call for a full and frank disclosure of medical history by a candidate to a potential employer seems unarguably right and should be encouraged. Under the Access to Health Records Act 1990, an individual is entitled to all recorded information about his or her health, but its disclosure to a potential employer must, of course, depend on the honesty of the applicant. There can be no question of direct access to records by a third party.

5.5.19 We were not constituted to be able, and have no mandate, to revise the rules of medical confidentiality. We may merely observe that it might be made a condition of employment in certain occupations, such as nursing, that candidates must themselves grant full access to all their medical history. Even here, we doubt the practicality of National Health Service managers or OH departments reviewing the entire medical history of every potential employee, in the search for reasons for disqualification. That would be a costly and time-consuming process and would lead to long delays in recruitment. An alternative and perhaps more practical approach would be to ask General Practitioners (GPs), with the candidate's consent, to certify that there is nothing in the candidate's medical history which would make them unsuitable for their chosen occupation. **We recommend** that consideration be given to how this might be achieved.

85

5.5.20   We interviewed Allitt's own GP with this proposition in mind. He doubted whether, if such a system had been in place when Allitt was recruited to Ward Four, he would have expressed any reservations about her suitability for employment as a nurse. She had consulted the practice 28 times in the three years she had been registered there. This was above average, but by no means exceptional. She had no history of psychiatric illness. Her GP had received discharge letters after each of her hospital attendances, but those letters, which we have seen, gave him no reason to suspect that the complaints for which she had received treatment were not genuine.

5.5.21   This evidence reinforces our belief that more thorough research into candidates' medical histories, even if it were feasible, would not necessarily reveal the presence of serious personality disorder, let alone a capacity for murder. All the expert evidence we have received confirms the common experience that psychopathic murderers show great ingenuity in concealing their intent. In recent years there have been many examples of the difficulty in the detection of serial killers.[3]

5.6   Role of the Physiotherapy Department

5.6.1   Throughout her training as a nurse, Beverly Allitt received treatment for her various injuries in the Physiotherapy Department at GKGH. It dawned gradually on her regular physiotherapist that Allitt did not always respond to treatment as she expected. She felt that something was not quite right, and was concerned about her. She surmised that Allitt was not continuing the exercises at home as instructed, and that she might deliberately be making her injuries worse. However, she seemed capable of looking after herself and the physiotherapist, who saw Allitt regularly over several years, did not conclude that her injuries were self-inflicted.

---

[3]In the evidence we heard from the Royal College of Nursing with regard to health screening, it was pointed out to us that there are no nationally agreed health criteria for the selection of qualified nurses or students.

5.6.2   A nurse has the primary responsibility of caring for patients. It is questionable whether someone with a morbid tendency to self-injury is a suitable person to care for others. For one thing it carries implications of deceitfulness. However, the physiotherapist herself did not regard nursing as an unsuitable career for her patient and, as we have found, she was not wholly convinced of the morbid tendency. However, she discussed her concerns with others involved in her care, but did not pass them on to the hospital management.

5.6.3   On the other hand, there were those in the Physiotherapy Department who were alarmed to discover that Allitt, with whom they were so familiar as a patient, was training to be a nurse. The Superintendent Physiotherapist decided that she should mention Allitt's repeated attendances to the Nurse Adviser. Her concern was not specific, but she felt that Allitt lacked the maturity of personality needed to care for others. She certainly did not predict the eventual outcome of Allitt's nursing career, but wanted to make sure that the management were aware of Allitt's medical history.

5.6.4   There is no written record of the meeting between the Superintendent Physiotherapist and the Nurse Adviser, or of any action taken thereafter. The Nurse Adviser felt sure that she would have passed on what she was told to the Senior Tutor at South Lincolnshire School of Nursing. We have been unable to verify what took place and certainly no further action was taken.

5.6.5   Since no written records exist, and the memories of those involved are not clear nearly five years after the event, we can take this no further. Nevertheless, it possibly represents a missed opportunity. The dismissal of pupil nurses simply on the basis of undefined concern expressed by other hospital staff would be quite unacceptable and would carry a strong risk of gross unfairness. But where concern is expressed, particularly by experienced clinical staff, steps should be taken to investigate the grounds for their concern.

5.7 Beverly Allitt's Behaviour on Ward Four

5.7.1   It is tempting, looking at the catalogue of attacks and murders and knowing who was responsible for the suffering and death of these children and babies, to believe that it must have been obvious that Beverly Allitt was seriously abnormal.   It seems inconceivable that someone capable of such unthinkable cruelty could appear to be a normal caring nurse. Somebody, one feels, should have realised she was very different.

5.7.2   However, having listened to nearly all of those who worked alongside Allitt, the overwhelming burden of the evidence was that she did indeed appear to be just like everybody else. She was friendly, willing and efficient, helpful to the student nurses, and well liked by other staff. Her colleagues knew about her health problems, but had no suspicion that they were self-inflicted.

5.7.3   A few of Allitt's colleagues noticed that she was unemotional, and that she didn't cry when children died, but they were in a minority.   Some noticed too that she did not pick babies up just to cuddle them in the way that most nurses did. But as one of her colleagues remarked, "I just thought that that was her way of handling the stress we all felt".   Lack of emotional expression is not unusual and some of us conceal our emotions under a mask of indifference.

5.7.4   One or two of the people we have interviewed said that it was no surprise, once they knew that someone was suspected of attacking the children, to find that it was Allitt. On the other hand, a greater number said they could not believe it until after she was convicted, and some did not believe it even then, still thinking there had been some terrible mistake⁴.

---

⁴It will have been noted that throughout our Inquiry, we sought always to draw evidence from the original sources, avoiding so far as possible hearsay and anecdote. Several of our witnesses referred to a journalist's account of the matter, "Murder on Ward Four", by Nick Davies, Chatto 1993, so we felt obliged to read it, but did not find it of help in reaching our conclusions. We were disturbed to read on page 345 this phrase about Beverly Allitt, "...she had littered the hospital with warning signs...". This assertion

5.8 Nurse Staffing Levels and Skill Mix on Ward Four

5.8.1   We have been advised that people who are determined to harm children can do so even on wards where the highest standards of care are maintained and where levels of staffing and provision of equipment are fully adequate. It takes only two minutes alone with an infant to cause death or serious injury. We must therefore begin this chapter with the caution that increasing the numbers of qualified staff on a ward may not be enough to prevent a tragedy such as this.

5.8.2   On the other hand, it seems reasonable to expect that the more qualified, permanent staff there are on a ward, the more closely a newly-qualified enrolled nurse such as Beverly Allitt will be supervised. We are in no doubt that Allitt was regularly permitted to undertake tasks and shoulder responsibilities that were quite inappropriate for someone at her level of training and experience. Furthermore, there is more time and opportunity in a well-staffed ward to take a step back and consider what might be causing an unusual series of events.

5.8.3   The nursing establishment determined by GKGH for Ward Four in January 1991 was 10.66 whole time equivalents (WTE). In other words, the number of nurses employed, whether full-time or part-time, was equivalent to 10.66 nurses working full-time. In addition there were some student nurses who, at that time, were included in the count of nurses available to provide the service.

---

we find to be as inaccurate as it is mischievous - the latter because it may lead the parents of the victims to believe that Allitt could very easily have been detected and stopped. Our careful researches have shown that not to be so.

The author twice emphasises that our Inquiry, not being set up under the Tribunals and Inquiries Act, 1992, had no power to compel attendance of witnesses or the discovery of documents. As was foreseen, every single witness whom we required to see attended and every document we wanted to see was produced. Witnesses spoke to us with a frankness impossible to find in a public arena. If we had needed further powers, we would have asked for and been given them by the Secretary of State.

Mr Davies seems to think that Trent Regional Health Authority settled our terms of reference. The truth is that they were settled by our Chairman. There seems no need to deal any further with the rest of the book.

On average there were four nurse learners on Ward Four. Despite clear national guidance on the importance of play and teaching staff, neither was employed on the ward during the period under consideration.

5.8.4   The actual number of staff in post on Ward Four was even lower than the funded establishment of 10.66 WTE. There were 8.86 WTE in January 1991, rising to 9.57 in February 1991 and falling again to 9.30 in March 1991. During the months in question there were only three full-time and one part-time nurse on Ward Four who held the qualification of Registered Sick Children's Nurse (RSCN) - that is to say 3.53 WTE of the funded establishment.

5.8.5   Most hospitals have a 'bank' of nurses who are available at short notice when individual wards need extra staff to cope with an increased workload or to cover for absence through sickness. One consequence of the shortage of staff on Ward Four was that nurses from the bank were increasingly needed to make up the required numbers. Some of the bank staff worked so often on Ward Four that they tended to be included on the monthly duty rota. Unfortunately only one of them was an RSCN.

5.8.6   Regular use of bank staff to fill funded vacancies is a matter of concern since it is detrimental to continuity of care and increases the possibility of failure of effective communication between colleagues. Attempts were made to recruit staff to fill the vacant posts, but without success.

5.8.7   There is no definitive guidance on the required establishment and skill mix for a 20 bed children's ward in a district general hospital. This is partly because of the number of variables involved. The Paediatric Nurse Managers Forum at the Royal College of Nursing carried out a project on staffing levels in 1989 and reached a consensus view that the minimum safe level was 24.00 WTE exclusive of play and teaching staff. Some Regional Nursing Departments issued staffing guidelines for patients in different age ranges and specialties. These guidelines have now been superseded since the introduction of various manpower planning methods. The formula used in the North Western Region, for example, would have recommended a minimum of 20.4 WTE for a ward such as Ward Four. With a total of 10.66 funded posts plus the four nurse learners, its establishment fell well below the above quoted figures.

5.8.8   The recommendation at the time in question was that there should be at least one RSCN on duty on children's wards throughout the 24 hour period. Subsequent guidance issued by the Department of Health during 1991 advised district health authorities and provider hospitals to take account of the following standard:

> "There are at least two RSCNs (or nurses who have completed the Child Health Branch of Project 2000) on duty 24 hours a day in all hospital children's departments and wards."[5]

We recommend that the Department of Health should take steps to ensure that this guidance is more closely observed.

5.8.9   In recent years there has been increasing emphasis on a family-centred approach to caring for children in hospital. By promoting the active participation of parents in the care of their children and providing them with teaching and support, wards are able to discharge children sooner. There is a higher throughput on children's wards and a concomitant reduction in length of stay. Children in hospital today are often acutely ill and require highly specialised nursing care and the use of sophisticated equipment. Bed occupancy in modern children's units is a less reliable indicator of workload than formerly and the need for a higher ratio of qualified to unqualified staff is of paramount importance.

---

[5]See paragraph 6.3 of the Department of Health guide, "Welfare of Children and Young People in Hospital", HMSO 1991.

5.8.10   In order to meet the requirement of one RSCN on duty in each ward at all times there need to be at least 6.0 WTE RSCNs in post. On Ward Four between January and April 1991 there were several shifts on day duty and two thirds of the night duty shifts when there was not an RSCN on duty. Indeed on some shifts an enrolled nurse was left in charge of the ward. Only one qualified nurse was on duty on a number of day shifts and on nearly all night shifts.

5.8.11   Several of the nurses we interviewed described problems caused by shortages of staff and the reliance on bank staff who were not always experienced in the care of children. One of the particular difficulties experienced at night, for example, was that the staff nurse on duty had to wait for the night sister in order to check medicines for the children. Sometimes this meant that medicines could not be given at the appropriate time. The night staff nurses discussed the situation with the night sisters.

5.8.12   In November 1990 Mrs Jean Savill, the Night Services Manager, requested a meeting with Miss Hannah Newton and Mrs Moira Onions, the nurse managers responsible for Ward Four, to discuss the problems on night duty. Mrs Savill met with the nurse managers on two occasions in January 1991. Mrs Onions also wrote to Miss Newton expressing concern about staffing levels at least twice. Despite all of the concern noted by the staff nurses and night sisters, little seems to have been done other than to approve additional bank staff when required to 'special' children. The difficulty with this arrangement was that very few of the bank staff were RSCNs and they were often not available at busy times and during holidays.

5.8.13   On 4th April 1991 Mrs Savill wrote again to Mrs Onions. The last paragraph of her letter read, "As the night duty nurse manager, I feel very distressed with the situation on Ward Four, and feel most strongly that being professionally accountable for these children in our care, I must voice my concerns in the

92

sincere hope that an early solution may be implemented before a tragedy occurs." The Tribunal acknowledges the notable efforts made by the late Mrs Jean Savill to improve staffing levels on Ward Four.

5.8.14   Nurse managers have been under increasing pressure in recent years to justify their requirements for nursing staff and to use systematic methods for agreeing the number and deployment of staff in all health care settings. In 1990 the majority of nurse managers were using or had access to one of the many recognised systems to aid manpower planning and justify the establishment and skill mix of nursing staff.

5.8.15   We understand that early in 1990 external consultants were commissioned to review the nurse staffing levels at GKGH. Unfortunately, Miss Newton did not take advantage of the consultants' expertise on behalf of the paediatric service. We are critical of the failure by the managers responsible for Ward Four to carry out any systematic review of the establishment and to present to the Unit General Manager, with supporting data, a clear case of need for an increase.

5.8.16   The overall result of the low staffing levels and inadequate number of qualified children's nurses on Ward Four was that, as we have stated earlier, Allitt was often one of only two qualified nurses on duty. This meant that she was left by the nurse in charge to 'special' ill children and frequently to escort them to Queen's Medical Centre (QMC) - a task usually allocated to a much more experienced nurse. Her colleagues did note that she was invariably present when a child collapsed, but they failed to attach any significance to the fact. Indeed, some of them teased her as an agent of bad luck. Nor were her colleagues particularly concerned about her undue self-confidence and apparent knowledgeability and her eagerness to accompany all of the children to QMC.

5.8.17   It is unlikely that, had there been more RSCNs and better continuity of care, Allitt would have been prevented altogether from attacking the children on Ward Four, but our findings suggest that the inadequacy of nurse staffing made it easy for her to fulfil her evil intent. It certainly contributed to the level of responsibility she was given and to the amount of time she spent unsupervised.

5.9 Medical Staffing of Ward Four

5.9.1   We must begin this section with the same caution as we did section 5.8: increasing the number of medical staff on the ward would not necessarily have prevented Beverly Allitt from committing her crimes, any more than would an increase in the number of qualified nurses. Indeed, if there had been more doctors involved in the care of Allitt's victims then the number of incidents observed by any single doctor would probably have been smaller. This might have meant it took longer before any of them began looking for a connection. On the other hand, if the doctors had been under less pressure from their day-to-day clinical responsibilities, they might have been in a better position to lift their heads and see the broader picture.

5.9.2   The medical establishment on the paediatric unit at GKGH consisted of two Consultant Paediatricians, Dr Porter and Dr Nanayakkara. Dr Nanayakkara had responsibilities in Newark in addition to his role in Grantham. He undertook four sessions a week fifteen miles away in Newark. The Consultants were supported by two Senior House Officers (SHOs), until a third SHO was appointed on 25th March 1991. All of these SHOs were on six month placements. SHOs came to GKGH with varying levels of experience in paediatrics. One of the posts was dedicated to a General Practitioner vocational training scheme. Trainees on this scheme often had no previous experience in paediatrics and were sent to Nottingham for a week's training at the beginning of their placement.

94

5.9.3   Between them, the Consultants and SHOs had to cover not only Ward Four, but also the Special Care Baby Unit and the Paediatric Out-patient Department which was situated on Ward Four.   They also had to be on hand if any problems arose with new-born babies in the maternity unit.   Until the third SHO was appointed, both Consultants and both SHOs were on call all day and on alternate nights during the week and alternate weekends, on a one in two rota.

5.9.4   Our impression is that the two Consultants were always willing to come in if the SHO on call needed assistance, so these inexperienced SHOs were not left to cope with unfamiliar situations alone.   We were also told that the Consultants maintained a high standard of teaching and training for the junior doctors, holding regular tutorials.   We noted the high standard of their record-keeping.   The nursing staff told us that the Consultants were invariably supportive and helpful to them, taking trouble to explain things at every opportunity.   It is not part of our remit to criticise the clinical judgment of the Consultant Paediatricians and we have found no grounds for doing so.

5.9.5   Nor is it for us to pronounce what the medical establishment on Ward Four should have been.   It is difficult to determine in a small hospital like GKGH how many medical staff are required to ensure that there is adequate on-call cover and that each doctor has enough work on a day-to-day basis to keep their skills up to date.   The two Consultant Paediatricians at GKGH had been pressing for several years for some middle grade support without success.

5.9.6   However, we are concerned that SHOs with as little as one week's experience in paediatrics should have been required to carry the responsibilities that they did.   Doctors in this position, and working a one in two rota, could not be expected to perceive the broad significance of all that was going on around them.   Equally, a consultant who is regularly on the ward out of hours to support inexperienced junior staff cannot be expected to take the same broad overall view as a consultant in a larger hospital, who is released to a certain extent from the stress and tiredness arising from this responsibility.

5.9.7   We can only speculate as to whether the two Consultants would have reacted more quickly and effectively to the series of collapses had they had more time to reflect.

5.10 Communication on Ward Four

5.10.1   In Chapter Four we reviewed the fragments of evidence which emerged over time pointing to the conclusion that the series of unexpected, life-threatening and sometimes fatal events which occurred on Ward Four was the result of criminal activity. Some of these fragments were overlooked until some time after the police investigation had begun. Others were recognised sooner, but by different individuals. Different members of staff were on duty when the various events occurred. Piecing together the overall picture depended on those individuals sharing the information they held.

5.10.2   On the basis of the evidence we have heard from the people who worked there during the relevant period, we believe that the general atmosphere on Ward Four was good. All those we have interviewed described it as a happy place to work. Most have said that they would have felt comfortable discussing any suspicions with senior staff. We have found no grounds for believing that any member of staff suspected that anyone was deliberately harming children on the ward.

5.10.3   However, as time went by the staff on Ward Four began to ask themselves and each other what might be causing so many children to suffer sudden cardio-respiratory arrests on the ward. Virtually all the staff appear to have discussed what was happening with others informally at one time or another. Each had their own ideas, but there was no forum in which they could work through the possibilities systematically.

5.10.4   We have already remarked that several of our witnesses supported our own common-sense belief that in the face of the succession of unexpected deaths and collapses on Ward Four, one would normally organise a multi-disciplinary conference to take time to consider the whole problem jointly and in the hope of sparking off ideas from all angles. We believe that if this had been done, there would have been a better chance that the culprit might have emerged.

5.10.5   However, where staffing levels are low and people therefore hard-pressed, time is a commodity in very short supply. Those of our witnesses who commended the idea of multi-disciplinary conferences in cases of death or complications mostly (but not invariably) came from large and well-established hospitals where there is a better possibility of standing back and looking at a problem. The immediate and often urgent demands of patient care tend, in a less well-endowed setting, to submerge reflection on grave matters in a sea of daily routine.

5.10.6   There seems to us little doubt that the insufficient staffing levels and inappropriate skill-mix on Ward Four at GKGH aggravated what we have seen as serious failures of communication which may have contributed to the delay in detecting and halting the criminal activity of Beverly Allitt. But there is evidence that there were other causes for these failures of communication.

5.10.7   Accusations have been made that the two Consultants did not communicate with one another, and that they would not listen to the views of the nursing staff. We have found very little evidence to support this view. It is true that their circumstances made communication difficult. The medical staffing situation described in section 5.9 above and Dr Nanayakkara's duties in Newark tended to mean that they were often not on duty together and were very busy whenever they were on duty.

5.10.8   There were instances where one or other of the Consultants did not hear about what had happened to a child for several days. We would not necessarily expect consultants to know all about what has happened to one another's patients, especially when they did not need to know for the purposes of continuation of treatment because the patient had been transferred to another hospital. On the other hand, faced with the emerging series of unexplained and unexpected life-threatening events, each of the Consultants appears to have pursued his own line of enquiry with inadequate reference to the other. Once they had begun looking for a connection between the various events, we would expect them to have sat down and exchanged what information they held about each of them. They did not do so until 22nd April.

5.10.9   The management structure of the ward may also have played a part in the failures of communication. Appendix 3 contains a simplified diagram representing the management structure for Ward Four. The Sister in charge was Sister Barbara Barker. Sister Barker was the only Sister on the Ward. She qualified as a Registered Sick Children's Nurse in 1975. Following a management re-organisation in 1989, Sister Barker reported to the Clinical Service Manager, Mrs Moira Onions. Mrs Onions was responsible for the day to day operational management of the Children's Ward and also for Gynaecology and Midwifery Services.

5.10.10   Mrs Onions in turn was responsible to Miss Hannah Newton, the Assistant General Manager (Maternity, Gynaecology and Children's Services), who had responsibility for the planning, management and development of children's services. Miss Newton was one of five Assistant General Managers (AGMs) who were members of the Hospital Management Group and reported directly to the Unit General Manager, Mr Martin Gibson. The Nurse Adviser for South Lincolnshire in 1991 was Mr Chris Pearce, who was also the Director of Nurse Education. Mr Pearce was responsible for the provision of professional nursing advice to the Authority but not for the management of nursing services, which had been devolved to hospital level.

5.10.11   Prior to 1989 Ward Four had been managed by the AGM for Patient Services who was responsible for all the general wards at GKGH.   A number of problems arose when the management structure changed. Miss Newton was based at the Pilgrim Hospital in Boston and was only able to visit GKGH once or twice a week. Both Miss Newton and Mrs Onions were experienced in the management of midwifery services but neither was a Registered Sick Children's Nurse.   In addition, the night staff on Ward Four were responsible to the general night sisters and not to the midwifery night sisters.   We noted with concern these arrangements for the management of Ward Four which resulted not only in a lack of communication but in staff feeling at times isolated from the rest of the hospital.

5.10.12   We are aware that in some hospitals the children's wards are included with maternity services within one management unit. All nurses should, however, have access to an experienced senior practitioner in their specialty for advice on professional issues.   Where such a person is not in post, there may be an increased risk that untoward incidents will not be recognised and monitored. We note with interest and endorse the recommendation in the recent Audit Commission Report, "Children First", that the management team should include, "a senior children's nurse above ward sister level, to provide the focus for implementing consistent policies for the care of children in all parts of the hospital".

5.10.13   Sister Barker was the most experienced nurse at GKGH who held a qualification in children's nursing.   Her role demanded therefore that she should be able both to function as the leader of the team on Ward Four and to supervise clinical standards of care and offer expert advice to her staff. We have heard evidence that Sister Barker did not function well in her role as leader.   She always made a point of accompanying the

Consultants on their ward rounds, but we find that she did not generally take the lead in supervising the ward. Less experienced staff were often left in charge while she carried out her administrative duties. Some of these, such as drawing up the off-duty rotas and finding extra bank staff, were routinely left to others.

5.10.14   When there is only one senior nurse in a specialty within a hospital it is essential that he or she is given every opportunity to attend relevant courses and conferences and to develop professionally. Although it appears that Sister Barker did have opportunities to maintain her knowledge and skills, she did not accept responsibility for passing them on to her colleagues and to the learner nurses on Ward Four. We have heard evidence, which we accept, that she did not take an interest in the training of learners. Indeed formal audits of the learning environment for students expressed concern about standards on Ward Four and threatened withdrawal of recognition.

5.10.15   Communication on the ward was not good and, although trained as a 'team briefer', it appears that Sister Barker did not promote the team briefing system in her ward. Despite the availability of a nurse with responsibility for quality management, there were no explicit nursing standards set for Ward Four. In addition the nursing records were of poor quality and showed little understanding of the nursing process.

5.10.16   The comments made in the preceding paragraphs are not meant as a criticism of the rest of the nursing staff on Ward Four who were, to a certain extent, 'caught up in the system'. The evidence showed that Sister Barker's relationship with her immediate manager, Mrs Onions, was strained and that she resented what she regarded as interference from her. A stronger management team might have been more effective in reviewing Sister Barker's performance and appointing someone with the ability and authority to bring policies and procedures up to date.

5.10.17   We were surprised to find that the incidents on Ward Four did not provoke collective management discussion to explore possible reasons for them, to re-examine procedures for coping with them and to give support to those distressed by them.   It seems possible that such reviews might have stimulated more curiosity about the observed fact that Allitt was the one nurse present on every occasion.   We doubt if she would have been able to provide satisfactory answers to detailed questions about the precise circumstances of the collapses.

5.10.18   Her recorded observations in the case notes would almost certainly have prompted enquiry.   The case of Katie Phillips illustrates this.   Allitt was with Katie at the time of her first collapse and she wrote in the notes, "Appeared blue and apnoeic".   On the second occasion, she wrote, "Crying++ colour suddenly went navy blue, gasping for breath", and later, "Screaming++ colour changed again to navy blue".   It is extremely rare for a baby without congenital heart disease suddenly to become 'navy blue', but the darkness of the colour was confirmed by others.   Allitt does not appear to have been asked for a more detailed description of what happened before Katie became blue.   We are surprised that Allitt was never subjected to close examination of what she had actually seen, although she was often the only person present, in any of the other episodes about which she first gave the alarm.   We are surprised also that no-one noticed some of the remarkable similarities in her descriptions of several of the various episodes when children collapsed.

5.10.19   In this section we have commented on the professional setting in which Allitt committed her crimes.   In a better staffed, better organised ward, with regular review of procedures and practices, we believe there might have been a better chance of earlier suspicion and detection of criminality.   But of this there can be no certainty.

5.11 Equipment on Ward Four

5.11.1   In addition to problems with staffing, it has been suggested that Ward Four had inadequate equipment. If the equipment for monitoring and resuscitation was not up to the required standard, children could have been put at risk. We therefore enquired into the provision of equipment, concerning ourselves particularly with the possible relevance of any deficiencies to the causation or outcome of any of the collapses, or to delay in detection of the person responsible for them.

5.11.2   Every ward at GKGH had a resuscitation trolley for use in emergencies which held all the basic equipment needed and a sealed box containing emergency drugs. The only piece of resuscitation equipment which was not on every ward was a defibrillator, which is used to apply electric shocks to the heart to restore normal rhythm. When a 'crash' call came from Ward Four, one of the hospital's three defibrillators had to be fetched from another department, together with special paddles for use on a child.

5.11.3   Bearing in mind that in normal circumstances it was very rare for the 'crash team' to be called to Ward Four, we do not regard the lack of a defibrillator as unreasonable. We have heard no evidence that resuscitation of any of the children on Ward Four was delayed because of the need to fetch equipment from elsewhere in the hospital. Neither have we heard evidence that shortage of other equipment had any direct bearing on the incidents themselves or on their outcomes.

5.11.4   Nevertheless, in the face of the critical events during the first three months of 1991, which resulted in no fewer than seven calls for the 'crash team', concerns were expressed about the adequacy of the equipment available to them. This issue was mentioned in Mrs Jean Savill's letter dated 4th April 1991 which we discussed in paragraph 5.8.13 and in an exchange of letters between Dr Nanayakkara and Dr Jean Breckenridge, the Consultant

Anaesthetist in Administrative Charge. However, these and other letters, although again signalling the degree of impoverishment of the ward, are not relevant to our Inquiry, addressing as they do preparedness to respond to the collapses rather than their cause.

5.11.5   There was one matter relating to equipment which was highly relevant to the circumstances of the collapses and about which we were greatly concerned. Seven of the children who collapsed were attached to monitors fitted with alarms which were set to go off if their breathing or heart beat slowed or stopped, or if oxygen saturation of the blood fell below a safe level. On at least four occasions, these alarms did not sound when the children collapsed, although they should have been triggered. The most likely explanation now appears to be that Allitt switched them off before attacking the children. Yet there was no investigation at the time as to why the alarms did not sound.

5.11.6   We heard in evidence from many of those who were called to resuscitate the children concerned that they were too busy with the child to worry about the failure of the alarm system. We accept this, but would have expected an inquiry into the fault to be instituted by the Ward Manager, Sister Barker, after the child was stabilised.   These alarms are designed to attract attention to a child as soon as an emergency arises and it is vitally important that they should not fail.   If someone had looked into why they did not sound and found no fault, suspicion might have been aroused, but no such examination was made. We recommend that in the event of failure of an alarm, an untoward incident report should be completed and the equipment serviced before it is used again.

5.12 Drug Security Procedures at GKGH

5.12.1   It is not known how Beverly Allitt obtained the drugs she used to attack the children on Ward Four.   In many cases, there is uncertainty as to which drug she used. We have heard expert evidence that it is possible to murder or seriously injure a child in a short space of time without any drug and without leaving marks on the child's body. Suffocation could produce effects similar to those seen in some of the children who collapsed. This may well have been the means used by Allitt in some cases. The implication of this is that even if she had had no access to drugs she might nevertheless have committed her crimes, albeit using different methods.

5.12.2   However, it remains true that by restricting unauthorised access to drugs we reduce the options available to someone like Allitt. The fact that she used a variety of methods to attack the children on Ward Four meant that they exhibited different symptoms. The reaction on Ward Four might have been quicker if every collapse had followed exactly the same course.

5.12.3   We must therefore review the drug security procedures at GKGH. We must explore whether Allitt might have abused the access to drugs she was legitimately given in the course of her work, or whether she might have obtained the drugs by some other means. We must also consider what mechanisms there were to monitor the use of drugs and to trigger a response if there was a sudden rise in the amount of, say, insulin or potassium used by any given ward.

5.12.4   Drug procedures at GKGH in 1991 were governed by the South Lincolnshire Health Authority Policy for the Care and Custody of Drugs, which came into force in February 1990. Whilst this appears to be a fairly clear and comprehensive policy, the version in force at the time of the incidents on Ward Four contained no reference to the importance of a Registered Sick Children's Nurse accepting responsibility for administration of medicines to children. Nor did the relevant policy on the Extended Role of the Nurse require an RSCN to give intravenous drugs to children. Of further concern was a memorandum attached to the Drug Policy which was issued on 10th May 1991. This memorandum sought to clarify the existing instructions on the role of the Nursing Auxiliary in relation to the administration of medicines including controlled drugs. In our view, this was in error since it contravened the guidance in the UKCC Advisory Paper on Administration of Medicines which was in existence at that time, and which is consolidated in the current UKCC Standards for the Administration of Medicines. We must however bear in mind that the policy was not designed, nor could we expect it to have been, to prevent nurses from using drugs to harm patients.

5.12.5   Each ward held stocks of drugs used regularly. The stock level was determined periodically through consultation between the Unit Pharmacist and the Ward Manager. As stocks were used, the empty containers were returned to the Pharmacy and replaced on a full for empty basis. Drugs designated as 'controlled drugs' by Act of Parliament, were stored and administered in accordance with the SLHA Policy.

5.12.6   Drugs were kept on Ward Four in locked cupboards in the Treatment Room or at the Nurses' Station. Some drugs were also kept on the drugs trolley. This was also locked, although we have heard that it was not always kept locked at night and we are critical of this practice. There was also a locked refrigerator for drugs, including insulin, which needed to be stored at low temperature. The keys for these cupboards were usually held by the nurse in charge of the ward, but the policy permitted them to depute their use to another nurse. Even an inexperienced enrolled nurse such as Allitt could be permitted to hold the keys for short periods. We know that Allitt did hold the keys on Ward Four on occasion.

5.12.7   The Policy for the Care and Custody of Drugs permitted enrolled nurses to administer medicines and stated the occasions on which a second qualified person (doctor or nurse) was required to check on all aspects of the procedure. We know that the enrolled nurses on Ward Four, including on occasion Allitt, did administer medicines. We could not however find any evidence that they had received additional instruction relevant to medicines encountered in paediatric practice nor had their knowledge and competence been assessed as recommended in the UKCC Advisory Paper, "Administration of Medicines". Accordingly we do not consider that Allitt should have been administering medicines without an RSCN or doctor being present. This would have made it difficult for her either to give the wrong drug or dose of drug deliberately or to steal a quantity of a drug while making it up legitimately for one patient for use later to harm another.

5.12.8   The only child to collapse while being given a drug was Michael Davidson. Allitt had helped the doctor giving it to make up the solution and she remained in the Treatment Room alone with the syringe while the doctor gave a drug to another patient. This was not in accordance with the policy, and it probably afforded Allitt the opportunity to tamper with the syringe intended for Michael.

5.12.9   We have noted that Allitt held the drug keys on occasion. She sometimes did so while the nurse in charge of the ward was having her meal break, leaving Allitt as the most senior nurse on the ward. It is possible that Allitt may have used the keys to remove drugs from the locked cupboards. It is difficult to see how such risk could have been avoided. It is essential that the nursing staff remaining on the ward during breaks have access to the drug cupboards. Nurses cannot and should not be expected to watch one another with suspicion at all times, and a qualified nurse has to be trusted with drugs. If nurses cannot trust one another the whole system becomes unworkable.

5.12.10   If Allitt was systematically removing phials of a drug, we might expect there to have been an increase in turnover of that drug on the ward which could have been picked up in the Pharmacy. The Pharmacy computer maintained a record of average issues of each drug to each ward. It would highlight instances where there was a sudden issue of more than the usual amount. The system was designed to adjust the supply of each drug, rather than to track the use of that drug. It did not show up any significant increases in the use of any drug on Ward Four during the period in question. The quantity of insulin used actually decreased.

5.12.11   It would in theory be possible to record in detail how every unit of every drug is used on a ward. But this would require keeping a record against the stock of precise quantities drawn up for administration to a patient or thrown away and of any loss or breakage. Every entry would need to be checked by two members of staff to make sure that nobody was falsifying the record. The system would be complicated by the fact that some patients, particularly those, such as diabetics, who receive regular medication, bring their own into hospital with them. The Unit Pharmacist at GKGH advised us that to make these checks on every drug would be an excessive administrative burden. We agree with him.

5.12.12   Allitt may have obtained the drugs from outside GKGH altogether. From March 1991 she was 'moonlighting' that is to say working additional shifts in nursing homes during her time off. It was stated at Allitt's trial that one of the nursing homes where she worked kept insulin in an unlocked refrigerator.

5.12.13   It is also possible that Allitt obtained insulin from elsewhere in GKGH. On 14th February 1991, she was handed the set of keys to fetch some eye-drops from the drug refrigerator. Shortly afterwards, Allitt reported that the key was missing. The keys were kept on a sturdy key ring. It is unlikely that the refrigerator key fell off accidentally. Despite an exhaustive search, it was never found. The lock was replaced the following day. We were surprised that we were unable to find an untoward incident report in respect of this incident.

5.12.14   The senior staff on Ward Four thought that by replacing the lock they had solved the problem, even if the key had been stolen. What they did not know was that all the refrigerators in the hospital at that time had the same lock.   The refrigerators were not designed to prevent access by staff from other wards. This fact was not discovered until after the police had been called to Ward Four. It is therefore possible that Allitt stole the key and used it to remove drugs from refrigerators on other wards.

5.12.15   We therefore conclude that the administration of drugs is yet another area in which closer observation of the proper procedures might have made it more difficult for Allitt to pursue her deadly course. In our view the administration of medicines to children should be under the direction of an RSCN. A local policy should state the circumstances which make the involvement of a second person desirable in the interests of patients. We welcome the development of self-administration of medicines and administration of medicines by parents to children where this is appropriate. A procedure to facilitate this should be included within the local policy. It is unlikely that tighter control over drugs would actually have prevented Allitt's crimes, but we have identified a number of opportunities to misuse drugs which she would not have had if the GKGH policy had been rigorously applied.

5.13 Role of Queen's Medical Centre, Nottingham

5.13.1   Seven of Beverly Allitt's victims were transferred to the intensive care unit at Queen's Medical Centre (QMC), Nottingham. One, Katie Phillips, was transferred to Nottingham City Hospital, but both the Senior Registrar who went to collect her from Grantham and the Consultant Paediatrician who took over responsibility for her care at the City Hospital also worked at QMC.   Both were involved in the care of other children transferred from Grantham. We must therefore review what part

QMC played in detecting that something untoward was happening to these children at GKGH, and whether they might have responded sooner.

5.13.2   The children's unit at QMC is a specialist unit which receives children referred from all over the surrounding area. Although all seven of the children who were transferred to QMC were received in the paediatric intensive care unit, at that time there was no consultant in overall charge of that unit. Children who were admitted to intensive care became the patients of different consultants. There were six consultant paediatricians in Nottingham in early 1991, working in three teams of two. One of those teams was based at the City Hospital.

5.13.3   The eight children transferred to Nottingham (including Katie Phillips at the City Hospital) were spread among these different teams.   One, Henry Chan, was the patient not of a consultant paediatrician but of a consultant neurosurgeon. The remaining seven were distributed among four Consultant Paediatricians.   In a large and busy hospital, we would not expect it to be immediately obvious to any of these individuals that there had been an increase in the number of transfers from GKGH.   On the other hand, the Locum Senior Registrar with responsibility for the Paediatric Intensive Care Unit from January to March, Dr Vibert Noble, admitted no fewer than five of the children.   He might have been struck by the quite exceptional flow of children from Grantham who had suffered collapses. As indicated in earlier sections, the circumstances of these collapses were in most cases unusual and we must examine individually their management in the specialist centre.

5.13.4   The first child to be transferred to Nottingham was Kayley Desmond on 9th March.   As we noted in paragraph 3.4.3, there was no reason to doubt at the time that her respiratory arrest had been the result of her inhaling her own vomit. She recovered quickly and the doctors at QMC saw no reason to be concerned about her after she returned to GKGH.   However, as already indicated in section 4.4 above, air in the right arm and axilla shown on chest x-ray, and later presumed to have been injected, was not observed by the Consultant in charge of her case and the x-ray was not reported on in the Radiology Department until its examination was requested by the police. Had the air been detected, its non-accidental introduction might have been suspected.

5.13.5   After Paul Crampton was transferred to QMC on 28th March, he was under the care of Dr Derek Johnston, a Consultant Paediatrician with special interest and expertise in endocrinology and in disorders of glucose metabolism. Because of his special knowledge, Dr Porter had consulted him by telephone about Paul whilst he was still in Ward Four. Dr Nanayakkara had suggested that Paul should be transferred to QMC because of the obscure nature of his attacks. Dr Porter was anxious to have Dr Johnston's opinion about the possible nature of the condition and also the desirability of transfer. At the time, Dr Johnston did not see any necessity for transferring the child.

5.13.6   When Paul eventually came under Dr Johnston's care, he was puzzled by the history of repeated episodes of hypoglycaemia. Paul suffered one further episode shortly after he arrived in Nottingham and a sample of his blood was taken for analysis. Dr Johnston arranged for insulin levels to be measured and he put in hand other biochemical investigations to exclude a number of rare metabolic disorders which can cause hypoglycaemic attacks. He knew that the child was not diabetic and did not consider the injection of insulin as a possible cause for his attacks.

5.13.7   Over the next few days the intravenous infusion of glucose that Paul had been receiving was stopped and the fact that he was able to tolerate its withdrawal without recurrence of hypoglycaemia reassured Dr Johnston that the child was unlikely to be suffering from an insulin-secreting tumour. He saw no need to keep Paul in hospital whilst awaiting the results

of the tests he had ordered. As he had apparently recovered
spontaneously, he allowed him to go home on 4th April, but with
the intention of following him up as an outpatient.

5.13.8   When the crucial insulin result was reported to Dr
Porter from Cardiff on 12th April (see section 4.11), he tried
to contact Dr Johnston for his advice. Unfortunately he was
unable to reach him and Dr Johnston went on holiday the next day,
remaining out of contact until 22nd April. Dr Johnston told us
that had he heard the results of the insulin assay and the c-
peptide estimations he would not have questioned their validity
and would have advised Dr Porter that the child must definitely
have been injected with insulin.

5.13.9   Although Dr Porter was unable to contact Dr Johnston
on 12th April, he did speak on the telephone to Dr Noble.
Although by this time Dr Noble had become a lecturer in
paediatrics and was primarily employed on a research project,
nevertheless he still took part in the rota for admissions to
QMC. He it was who admitted five of the Grantham children who
were transferred as emergencies. He did not advise Dr Porter as
Dr Johnston told us he himself would have done. Dr Noble
expressed the view that it would be wrong to place reliance on
a single result, notwithstanding the special expertise of the
laboratory whence it came. He told Dr Porter that he would
arrange for the assays to be repeated on a sample of Paul's blood
taken after his transfer to QMC.

5.13.10   Dr Noble made a note of what Dr Porter had said in Paul
Crampton's medical records and he also recorded the result of the
insulin assay on the sample of Paul's blood taken at QMC on 28th
March. It had been carried out in the QMC laboratory and showed
a level of 148 mU/l. It is not clear when this result was first
available as the original report slip was mislaid. Although not
as high as the result Dr Porter had reported, it was six times
greater than the normal level. The laboratory had not been
instructed to measure c-peptide, but given Paul's spontaneous

recovery, it was unlikely that the insulin measured was endogenous.

5.13.11   On Tuesday 16th April 1991, Dr Noble wrote to the Clinical Biochemist at Nottingham asking him to measure the c-peptide level in the sample of Paul's blood that had been sent to him. He in turn referred it to the Cardiff laboratory, where it arrived on 26th April.   The result confirmed the raised insulin level, though at a slightly lower level than had been found in Nottingham, and a low c-peptide. Dr Porter was advised of this result by telephone on 3rd May with confirmation by letter on 8th May.   There had been every reason to ensure that this test was carried out with urgency, but instead it was handled as a routine sample.

5.13.12   Dr Noble's response compounded the uncertainty in Dr Porter's mind as to the interpretation of the first result from Cardiff on 12th April. Although Dr Noble himself felt that too much reliance should not be placed on the Cardiff result, he told us that he did pass on the information to Dr Johnston's medical team and he assumed that they would be following up the matter. He told us that it was the result of the assays on Paul Crampton's blood that triggered the concern of the QMC doctors and encouraged them to look back at all the cases they had received from Grantham.

5.13.13   Although there is some uncertainty as to who told what to whom at QMC about Paul Crampton's insulin and c-peptide levels, it is beyond dispute that the critical information was passed to QMC on 12th April, and that advice was sought on its interpretation. There were experts at QMC at the time who have confirmed to us that there was only one possible interpretation, namely, that insulin had been administered to the child, an event which should have demanded urgent investigation possibly involving Child Protection Services.

112

5.13.14   Bradley Gibson was transferred to Nottingham on 30th March, less than 48 hours after Paul Crampton. Like Paul's, his case was odd. The history of his cardiac arrest did not fit with his previous illness. Dr Terence Stephenson, the Consultant Paediatrician in charge of his care, did not believe that he collapsed as a result of his asthma. He suspected that Bradley had been given the wrong drug, or a drug in the wrong dose or by the wrong route. However, when the night sister at GKGH confirmed that Bradley was not receiving any drug when he collapsed, Dr Stephenson did not pursue the matter further.

5.13.15   The night sister at GKGH did not record her conversation with Dr Stephenson in the notes or pass on what was said to Dr Porter, who had been responsible for Bradley's care. Had Dr Porter known that Dr Stephenson thought that a drug error was the most likely explanation for what happened, it might have led to earlier detection of mischief. Both Dr Porter and Dr Nanayakkara told us that no-one at QMC communicated to them any concern about Bradley Gibson. Dr Stephenson stated that he remained puzzled by Bradley's history and mentioned to Dr Nanayakkara, whom he met on 5th April at a conference, that he found the case very odd. Dr Nanayakkara did not recall that conversation.

5.13.16   Dr Stephenson did not of course realise at the time how close he was to the dreadful truth that Bradley's heart attack had indeed been caused by a drug. It is understandable that he did not tell Dr Porter or Dr Nanayakkara that he had considered and excluded the possibility of drug error, at least to his own satisfaction. We were told that a Consultant Anaesthetist in the Intensive Care Unit commented as an aside about ·Bradley's case that, "This is the sort of thing that happens when potassium is injected". No doubt because it seemed so improbable, this comment stimulated no further thought or action.

5.13.17   Henry Chan was transferred to Nottingham on 31st March. Because of his head injury, he was transferred to the care of a consultant neurosurgeon, rather than one of the paediatricians. A CT scan showed a small haemorrhage in the brain. It seemed perfectly reasonable to conclude that this had caused him to suffer seizures at GKGH.

5.13.18 After she collapsed on 7th April, Katie Phillips was taken not to QMC but to Nottingham City Hospital. She was in a critical condition when the team from Nottingham went to collect her from GKGH. Like Bradley Gibson, she became Dr Stephenson's patient. Dr Stephenson found Katie's illness less puzzling than Bradley's. He knew that she was a twin born prematurely with a low birth weight and that her twin sister had died suddenly. It seemed likely that they had both been affected by the same metabolic disorder or infection. Dr Stephenson carried out extensive investigations, but he could not find anything to explain what had happened.

5.13.19 Katie responded well to treatment in Nottingham and was well enough to be transferred back to GKGH just over a week later. The cause of Katie's illness had not been diagnosed, but the worst seemed to be over. We do not forget that doctors not infrequently fail to reach a diagnosis. We have already discussed, in section 4.9 above, the fact that rib fractures which were later discovered on x-rays of Katie's chest were not detected at this time, despite the fact that the films were reported in the Radiology Departments at GKGH and the City Hospital. We were told by an expert witness that fractures of the type shown were usually caused by the shaking of an infant held by the chest. They were not characteristic of injuries sustained during cardio-pulmonary resuscitation. Again, a clue to probable child abuse had been missed, but the radiological changes were inconspicuous and easily overlooked.

5.13.20 Christopher Peasgood, Christopher King and Patrick Elstone were all transferred to QMC within a week of each other, between Saturday 13th April and Thursday 18th April. They had all stopped breathing suddenly at GKGH and had become blue.

Christopher Peasgood and Christopher King both recovered quickly and were discharged home after three and five days respectively. Patrick Elstone suffered seizures at Nottingham and was kept in until 29th April.

5.13.21   Following these later episodes, some of the doctors in Nottingham, discussing their cases informally, realised that many of the cases which worried them were transfers from GKGH. They met together on Monday 29th April. On the previous Friday Professor Sir David Hull, the senior Consultant Paediatrician at QMC, became aware of the children who had been transferred from GKGH, none of whom had been his patient. In particular, he was alarmed to hear of the results of the tests on Paul Crampton's blood. He instigated the meeting on 29th April and asked for a report of the findings.

5.13.22   At the meeting, the cases of Paul Crampton, Bradley Gibson, Katie Phillips, Christopher King and Patrick Elstone were discussed. Even at this stage, there was no suspicion about what had happened to Kayley Desmond or Christopher Peasgood. The meeting did not find anything common to the five cases they discussed, but they concluded that, "It is very clear, however, that all of these children have had a clinical course completely out of context to their presenting illness and we are concerned that there may be an extrinsic factor which has changed their clinical course".

5.13.23   A written record of the discussion was produced the same day and passed to Professor Sir David Hull, who telephoned Dr Porter to find out what was happening at GKGH. In the course of this conversation, he advised him to call the police. The next day Sir David telephoned to check whether Dr Porter had followed his advice and was told that the police had been called.

5.13.24   Dr Porter told us that he spoke to Sir David Hull at the BPA conference on 16th or 17th April. He was sure he would have mentioned the result of the insulin assay on Paul Crampton's blood. Sir David told us that he might have had a conversation with Dr Porter at that conference, but that he was not aware of any untoward incidents in Grantham as a result. He was not aware of the results of the analysis of Paul Crampton's blood until 26th April.

5.14 Roles of South Lincolnshire Health Authority and Trent Regional Health Authority

5.14.1   Paragraph 1.5 of our terms of reference requires us "to advise on the most efficient way for Health Authorities to be informed of serious untoward incidents and to monitor their handling; and to consider whether and, if so, how the Regional Health Authority should be informed of serious untoward incidents and the way in which they are handled". There have been a great many changes in the structure of the NHS in recent years. It was announced while our Inquiry was in progress that further changes are contemplated, leading eventually to the abolition of Regional Health Authorities. We agree that serious untoward incidents must be monitored from outside the management structure of individual hospitals. However, in the present state of transition it is difficult to judge where responsibility should lie for such monitoring and what systems will be most appropriate to ensure that the function is carried out efficiently.

5.14.2   Against this background, we do not consider that our Inquiry has put us in a position to design an efficient system for reporting and monitoring serious untoward incidents, but we would make the following observations. Definition of a serious untoward incident is elusive. Ultimately, the judgment as to whether an incident is sufficiently grave to be reported to a higher authority has to be made at local level. Guidelines can give examples of the type of incidents which should be reported, but cannot be exhaustive. There will always be new situations or borderline cases where a judgment has to be made.

5.14.3   In recent years there has been growing interest, both theoretical and practical, in matters relating to quality in health services provision. This 'quality initiative' was given fresh impetus by the National Health Service and Community Care Act 1990, which introduced explicit contractual arrangements between purchasers and providers of services. Quality measures embody a number of systems and procedures, including critical incident review, which go to the setting of standards and the monitoring of their achievement. It is likely that within the scope of this initiative guidelines on response to untoward events will be developed. The ever increasing sophistication of information systems will help to facilitate the establishment of robust procedures.

5.14.4   By agreement with the Department of Health and Trent Regional Health Authority, we therefore confine the review which follows to when and how South Lincolnshire Health Authority (SLHA) and Trent Regional Health Authority (Trent RHA) were informed of the events on Ward Four and what action they took after they had been informed.

5.14.5   Mr Malcolm Townson, the District General Manager of South Lincolnshire Health Authority, first heard about the events on Ward Four on Tuesday 23rd April. He had attended meetings at GKGH about other matters over the preceding weeks, but he was not told about collapses on Ward Four. During the course of a routine telephone conversation on 23rd April, the Unit General Manager Mr Gibson told Mr Townson about Dr Porter's telephone call on Friday 19th April and the ensuing discussions (See paras 4.16.5 to 4.16.7). Mr Gibson explained that Dr Porter feared that a child on Ward Four had been injected deliberately with insulin, but added that it was not yet clear whether his fears were justified. He said that he would keep Mr Townson informed.

5.14.6   Mr Gibson did not ask or expect Mr Townson to take any action in response to what he told him. It might be said that Mr Townson should have made sure that Dr Porter's fears were fully investigated as quickly as possible, but we are not convinced that there is ground for criticism here. Mr Townson had been informed in passing of something which, at that stage, Mr Gibson himself doubted would turn out to be true. Unhappily, Dr Porter had acquired a reputation for raising alarms which turned out to be unjustified (see paragraph 4.16.5) and in the circumstances it is not surprising that neither Mr Gibson nor Mr Townson thought it necessary to intervene at this stage, but preferred to wait for corroboration of what Dr Porter had said.

5.14.7   Apart from a brief exchange with Dr Porter outside Mr Gibson's office on 29th April, when Dr Porter was waiting to see Mr Gibson, Mr Townson heard nothing more about the events on Ward Four until the morning of 30th April. After he had called the police, Mr Gibson rang Mr Townson to inform him. Mr Townson suggested that a clinician from elsewhere be invited to conduct a medical audit in parallel with the police investigation and took responsibility for organising this in consultation with the Regional Medical Officer. From that point on, Mr Townson and SLHA were closely involved in the handling of the investigation.

5.14.8   No report of untoward incidents on Ward Four reached Trent Regional Health Authority until Tuesday 30th April, after the police had been called. Dr Porter telephoned Trent RHA that afternoon in the hope of speaking to Dr (now Professor) Richard Alderslade, the Regional Director of Public Health and Regional Medical Officer. Dr Alderslade was unavailable, so a lengthy explanation was given to a senior manager in the Regional General Manager's Department. She spoke to Mr Gibson immediately after this conversation to find out his view of the situation and passed on what she had been told to Dr Alderslade and to the Regional Legal Adviser. From that point on Trent RHA too was closely involved.

5.14.9   Earlier in April, Dr Alderslade had attended several meetings at GKGH to discuss junior medical staffing and the development of the link between Grantham and Newark. After a meeting on 11th April, Dr Porter and Dr Nanayakkara showed Dr Alderslade around Ward Four. As they did so, they mentioned that there had been an unusually high number of collapses on the ward in recent weeks. Dr Alderslade asked their opinion of the cause and they told him it might be a virus.

5.14.10   We do not believe that this constituted reporting of a serious untoward incident to the RHA. The Consultant Paediatricians did not express concern to Dr Alderslade about the cause of the collapses. He believed that their reason for telling him was to show that the ward needed more staff and equipment, which was what had been discussed at the meeting. The matter was not raised with Dr Alderslade again before 30th April.

5.14.11   It appears, therefore, that neither South Lincolnshire Health Authority nor Trent Regional Health Authority was informed of a serious untoward incident on Ward Four until after the police were asked to investigate. It is difficult to see how they might have been informed sooner, since nobody at GKGH appears to have been convinced before then that anything untoward had happened. The problem was not with communication between GKGH and SLHA and Trent RHA, but with communication within GKGH.

5.14.12   One general conclusion we can draw from this experience is that health authorities should make clear that, once the judgment has been made that a serious untoward incident should be reported, a casual mention in passing does not constitute reporting of that incident. It should be emphasised that, although a telephone call may be a sufficient initial warning of such an incident, it must always be followed by a written report, however brief. Moreover, the simple act of telling someone else of one's concerns does not absolve one of taking action oneself. It is the responsibility of the individuals involved to make sure they know at the end of a conversation of this kind what action each proposes to take. We do not wish to inhibit informal communication between hospitals and district and regional health authorities (and their successors), but we recommend that reports

of a serious nature should be made in writing and through a
single channel which is known to all involved.

CHAPTER SIX: THE REGIONAL FACT FINDING INQUIRY INTO PAEDIATRIC SERVICES AT GKGH

6.1 We have already noted that the terms of reference of the Committee of Inquiry into Paediatric Services at GKGH specifically excluded any retrospective review. The purpose of that Inquiry was to review existing practices at GKGH. The Committee of Inquiry began its work in January 1992 and reported in July 1992. Many changes had already been made to the paediatric service at GKGH since the events of February to April 1991 and further changes have been made since May 1993, when the management of the service was transferred to Queen's Medical Centre in Nottingham.

6.2 Our own terms of reference require us to review the recommendations of that Committee of Inquiry and to advise whether any additions or amendments to those recommendations are necessary. We must stress that we have not ourselves reviewed the current state of paediatric services at GKGH. We can only advise on whether our own findings in respect of the events on Ward Four in February to April 1991 support those recommendations.

6.3 The Regional Inquiry made a total of 51 recommendations in relation to the management of both paediatric and neonatal services at GKGH. We have reviewed these recommendations, some of which concern aspects of the service which were not material to our Inquiry. Since our Inquiry was confined to the events which occurred on Ward Four we felt unable to comment on those which related to the neonatal service.

6.4 In general terms we support the remaining recommendations with the exception of Number 233, with which we differ. This recommendation states, "The Recruitment Policy for the hospital should specifically state that where only one reference for nurses is being obtained this should be a work related one". In our own recommendations we state, "We recommend that, for all those seeking entry to the nursing profession, in addition to routine references, the most recent employer or place of study should be asked to provide at least a record of time taken off on grounds of sickness". The reasons for this have been explained in section 2.4.

6.5 A small number of the recommendations fall within the remit of the General Manager at GKGH and two relate to Mid-Trent College of Nursing and Midwifery. The remainder have been reviewed by the managers of Queen's Medical Centre. We have received from each of these authorities a report describing in detail their response to each of the recommendations. It is reassuring to note that many of the suggested changes have already been made and the rest are in the process of being made or are currently under review. In the light of our comments on the serious understaffing which prevailed at the time, we are pleased to note the substantial increase recommended in both medical and nurse staffing levels.

6.6 We also welcome the firm recommendations with regard to the need to extend the procedure for checking whether nurses who are liable to come into contact with children have a criminal background and for ensuring that accurate records are maintained of the qualifications and registration status of all nursing staff. We commend the priority given to implementing these two recommendations and emphasise the importance of all employers using the UKCC's confirmation service to confirm that the claimed registration of nurses is valid, and that they possess a current and effective registration. It should be noted that the UKCC now has the power to impose interim suspension of a practitioner's registration. This power, however, can only be effective in protecting the public if employers avail themselves of the Council's confirmation service.

6.7 We have made a number of additional recommendations as a result of our own Inquiry. These recommendations are summarised in Chapter Seven below.

CHAPTER SEVEN: SUMMARY OF CONCLUSIONS AND RECOMMENDATIONS

7.1 In the course of our Inquiry we have interviewed 94 witnesses and have read many thousands of pages of documentary evidence of one sort or another. We have found that, as is the case in nearly all human catastrophes, there were many factors that contributed to the totality of this disaster. Central to it was, of course, Allitt herself. Without her grotesque and almost unique proclivities the tragedy would not have occurred. But she was admitted to and operated within an environment which somehow afforded her the scope and opportunity to perpetrate her crimes. It is this environment, and those who populated it, that we have been required to examine to try to identify mistakes or weaknesses that might have contributed to, or at least failed to contain, the enormity of the disaster. And we have been required to do so at a level of thoroughness that would have found few institutions, subjected to such scrutiny, without fault or flaw.

7.2 Allitt's nefarious activities extended over a period of two months. We have been critical, as have others, of the delay in recognising that a criminal force lay behind the series of collapses on Ward Four. But we are mindful that in the rare previous reports of serial killing in hospital, the delays in detection were very much greater. The human mind takes time to grasp a reality that is totally beyond its experience or its comprehension. We are also mindful of the evidence presented to us repeatedly that in whatever hospital setting Allitt had found herself, from the lowliest to the most prestigious, she would almost certainly have secured the means to satisfy her urge. It was the sad misfortune of GKGH to be the scene of her crimes.

7.3 We learned from several witnesses and from perusal of a number of reports that GKGH was poorly endowed, particularly in terms of staffing levels, and that this reflected the size of its catchment area and its patient turnover. Indeed, we were told that in these respects it was on the borderline of viability. We recognise that there are often powerful pressures to retain hospitals in this predicament for proper reasons of civic pride and local need. But we conclude that if the decision is taken to retain such hospitals, it must be accepted that staffing and other norms cannot be applied rigidly, that lower levels of cost effectiveness are to be expected and that appropriate funding must therefore be made available. These comments do not, of course, exonerate GKGH from the criticisms we have made, but are intended to put them in context.

7.4 Although at one remove from the scene of the crimes, the two highly specialised and well-endowed paediatric departments in Nottingham were also involved in the tragedy. They admitted eight children referred from Grantham. They too had a view of a series of unexpected and in most cases unexplained events although through a narrower window. Perhaps the divided responsibility lowered the index of suspicion at both ends. The junior staff at Queen's Medical Centre did notice that the numbers of collapsed children arriving from Grantham were well in excess of what might have been expected. Eventually their observations, translated into action by Sir David Hull, played an important part in halting the train of events. Even so, the point is made that in the best regulated circumstances it still took time to adjust to realities that were far outside routine expectation - time during which important clues were missed.

7.5 The criticisms we have made in the body of our report fall roughly into two categories: those that relate to attitudes and procedures that prevailed during the early months of 1991 in the hospitals concerned, and to individual and collective responses to events; and secondly, those that derive from loss or oversight of specific clues that might, had they been recognised, have led to earlier awareness of criminal influence. There is, of course, considerable overlap between these two categories.

7.6 We summarise below what we see as the main failures which contributed to vulnerability to outrage or incapacity to contain it.

a)   The background to the employment of Beverly Allitt as an enrolled nurse was unsatisfactory. Her health record was disregarded, and referral for its assessment by the Occupational Health Department, the agency set up for the purpose, was neglected. The managerial procedures relating to the appointment itself were sloppy.

b)   Nurse staffing levels on Ward Four, both in terms of numbers and experience, were inadequate. Nevertheless, the nurses who served on the ward did so with care and dedication. What they lacked was leadership and example. We have severely criticised the Ward Manager and those to whom she was responsible for a variety of failures, not least for dilatory and ineffective action when apprised of suspicions of foul play.

c)   We have also criticised senior management in the hospital for a general laxity of operational procedures within its responsibility and for indecisiveness in the later stages of the crisis.

d)   We have commended the two Consultant Paediatricians for their skill and dedication, for their teaching of junior doctors and nurses and for the standard of their record-keeping.   We have recognised that consultant staffing was inadequate and lacking in support by junior doctors, in both numbers and experience. Nevertheless, we have criticised them for their failure to grasp sooner than they did the significance of the cascade of collapses with which they had to deal. Some of our witnesses told us that the exceptional number of cases, far in excess of routine expectation, should have prompted them to early and vigorous investigation in search of a common cause. Others told us that it was detailed consideration of the unusual clinical features of individual cases that should have alerted them to the mischief that was afoot. Either way, we contend that if a meeting involving staff in all disciplines had been convened, as it should have been as soon as the chance determination of events began to strain credulity, there is a strong likelihood that their malevolent cause would have been detected.

e)   Given the high standards attainable at Queen's Medical Centre (QMC), similar criticism might be levelled. But although there too the flow of referrals from a single source was quite exceptional, the greater number of staff and their disposition in three separate teams diluted the experience of each. The maximum number of cases seen by one individual member of staff was five.

f)   There were circumstances relating to the death of one child that do call for serious adverse comment. It is of particular significance that this was the first child in the series of victims. We had evidence that the Consultant in charge of the case made a determined effort to have a post mortem carried out by a paediatric pathologist. He was thwarted by the combined efforts of the locum general pathologist and the Coroner's Officer in circumstances that are not entirely clear, since their evidence was conflicting. The post mortem findings were in fact inexplicable. Their mysterious nature was conveyed to the Coroner but he accepted death as being due to natural causes. There is a distinct possibility that had the Consultant Paediatrician been listened to, the whole train of events might have been brought to a halt as a result of this first incident.

g)   There were two other cases in which the same locum pathologist recorded a cause of death which, in retrospect, was unsatisfactory. In one the death was attributed to

126

"status epilepticus", although the clinical evidence was that the child was not having seizures at the time of death. In the second, Sudden Infant Death Syndrome was the certified cause, although uncharacteristically there was evidence of illness and distress during the evening prior to death. The pathologist himself told us that he was not entirely satisfied with these diagnoses. However, any pathologist must make a judgment on the balance of probabilities in the light of the pathological findings and the clinical history, neither of which gave a clear indication of the cause of death in either of these cases. It is understandable, though regrettable, that the possibility of foul play was not considered in these two cases.

h)   We have described in detail the clue which ultimately led to recognition of criminal behaviour, namely the grossly abnormal insulin level in one of the children. But we have deplored the ineptitude of the responses to this vital piece of intelligence, particularly at GKGH but to a lesser extent also at QMC. There was a delay of over two weeks between the first arousal of suspicion of foul play in the mind of the Consultant Paediatrician, and the involvement of the police. During this period another child died. The Consultant was ill-served by the advice he sought and by the response of managers to his requests for action.   Nevertheless he himself was indecisive and ineffective in following up the vital clue.

i)   In two of the children, both of whom survived Allitt's assault, there were abnormalities in the chest x-rays which were missed by clinicians both in Grantham and Nottingham. They only came to light in the course of the police inquiry when a radiologist was asked to review all relevant films. In the case of one of the children, there were rib fractures which he deemed to have been due to violence. In the other there were shadows in the arm and axilla which,

127

in retrospect, could only be interpreted as due to malicious injection of air. Had either of these abnormalities been detected at the appropriate time, they would have provided powerful evidence of non-accidental, ie criminal, injury. Their oversight by the clinicians who saw the x-rays, and who would certainly be concentrating on the appearances of the lungs, was understandable. But the fact that the latter x-rays were not seen or reported in the Radiology Department at QMC suggests a failure in practice or procedure.

7.8 In these paragraphs we have identified what we see as the main failures and objects of criticism in this grievous story. They vary in significance in terms of their contribution to the delay in bringing it to an end. No single circumstance or individual can be held responsible for what happened. But taken together, the catalogue of lapses from the high standards to which the National Health Service aspires point to lessons which should be heeded if every effort is to be made to contain such a catastrophe should it strike again. In light of these lessons we make the following recommendations:

1)   **We recommend** that, for all those seeking entry to the nursing profession, in addition to routine references the most recent employer or place of study should be asked to provide at least a record of time taken off on grounds of sickness (para 2.4.4).

2)   **We recommend** that in every case Coroners should send copies of post mortem reports to any consultant who has been involved in the patient's care prior to death whether or not demanded under Rule 57 of the Coroner's Rules 1984 (para 4.2.9).

3)   **We recommend** that the provision of paediatric pathology services be reviewed with a view to ensuring that such services be engaged in every case in which the death

of a child is unexpected or clinically unaccountable, whether the post mortem examination is ordered by a Coroner or in routine hospital practice (para 4.2.16).

4)   **We recommend** that no candidate for nursing in whom there is evidence of major personality disorder should be employed in the profession (para 5.4.11).

5)   **We recommend** that nurses should undergo formal health screening when they obtain their first posts after qualifying (para 5.5.13). We acknowledge that in Allitt's case this was done.

6)   **We recommend** that the possibility be reviewed of making available to Occupational Health departments any records of absence through sickness from any institution which an applicant for a nursing post has attended or been employed by (para 5.5.14).

7)   **We recommend** that procedures for management referrals to Occupational Health should make clear the criteria which should trigger such referrals (para 5.5.14).

8)   **We recommend** that further consideration be given to how the suggestion of the Chairman of the Association of NHS Occupational Physicians (see para 5.5.16) could be applied in practice (para 5.5.17).

9)   **We recommend** that consideration be given to how General Practitioners might, with the candidate's consent, be asked to certify that there is nothing in the medical history of a candidate for employment in the National Health Service which would make them unsuitable for their chosen occupation (para 5.5.19).

10) **We recommend** that the Department of Health should take steps to ensure that its guide, "Welfare of Children and Young People in Hospital", is more closely observed (para 5.8.8).

11) **We recommend** that in the event of failure of an alarm on monitoring equipment, an untoward incident report should be completed and the equipment serviced before it is used again (para 5.11.6).

12) **We recommend** that reports of serious untoward incidents to District and Regional Health Authorities should be made in writing and through a single channel which is known to all involved (para 5.14.12).

13) The foregoing recommendations are aimed at the tightening of procedures to safeguard children in hospital. But no measures can afford complete protection against a determined miscreant. **The main lesson from our Inquiry and our principal recommendation is that the Grantham disaster should serve to heighten awareness in all those caring for children of the possibility of malevolent intervention as a cause of unexplained clinical events.**

EPILOGUE

Whenever some great disaster befalls the human race, the instinctive reaction of most people is to seek its cause and try to prevent a recurrence. But behind this civilized response there lies a darker motivation as old as time - the urge to lay blame. The ancient notion of a scapegoat, to bear the guilt for disastrous happenings and thus relieve feelings of rage and frustration, is still with us.

Where we have found culpability, we believe that we have placed it firmly where it belongs. But those whom we have criticised were subjected by chance to a test more severe than any which most of us encounter in a lifetime: so we have not striven to find fault merely to satisfy a popular urge to see suffering in others as the proper response to one's own.

We were struck throughout our Inquiry by the way in which fragments of medical evidence which, if assembled, would have pointed to Allitt as the malevolent cause of the unexpected collapses of children, lay neglected or were missed altogether. Taken in isolation, these fragments of medical evidence were not all very significant nor was the failure to recognise some of them very culpable. But collectively they would have amounted to an unmistakeable portrait of malevolence. The principal failure of those concerned lay in not collecting together those pieces of evidence. The initiative and the energy needed to do this were not forthcoming at GKGH. That is the true and ultimate criticism.

Civilised society has very little defence against the aimless malice of a deranged mind. Wherever we have found the slightest possibility of prevention, we have pointed to it. The tightening of standards which we have sometimes urged must be a good in itself and such small improvements may reduce the opportunities open to another Beverly Allitt.

LIST OF WITNESSES AND SUBMISSIONS TO THE INQUIRY

WITNESSES

Teaching Staff:

Charles Read School, Corby Glen

Mr J Gleeson - Headteacher
Mrs B M Goodjohn - Deputy Head Teacher

Grantham College of Further Education

Mrs R Barber - Tutor

South Lincolnshire School of Nursing (now Mid Trent College of Nursing and Midwifery)

Ms D Grieve - Senior Tutor (in writing)
Mr R Pitt - Nurse Tutor
Mrs K Shelbourn - Nurse Tutor

Pilgrim Hospital

Ms H Sharples - Nurse Tutor

Staff of Grantham and Kesteven General Hospital:

Managers

Mr R P Arnett - Director of Personnel
Mr P Flood - Assistant General Manager
Mr E M Gibson - Unit General Manager
Mr S Harrison - Clinical Services Manager

Mrs B Hutchinson - Assistant General Manager/ Nurse Adviser (retired)

Miss H Newton - Clinical Services Manager (based at Pilgrim Hospital, Boston)

Mrs D M Onions - Clinical Services Manager

Mrs S Slee - Clinical Services Manager

Mr R Thompson - Senior Pharmacist

Medical Staff

Dr K Bradshaw - Junior House Officer General Surgery

Dr J L Breckenridge - Consultant Anaesthetist

Dr C S Livingstone - Locum Consultant Paediatrician

Dr T Marshall - Locum Consultant Pathologist

Dr C S Nanayakkara - Consultant Paediatrician

Dr F N Porter - Consultant Paediatrician

Dr M Ratnayaka - Paediatric Senior House Officer

Dr H Tailor - Paediatric Senior House Officer

Nursing staff

Mrs B Asher - Enrolled Nurse

Miss B Barker - Ward Sister

Miss S Biggs - Student Nurse

Miss C Cooper - Student Nurse

Mrs J Cottam - Staff Nurse

Mrs D Fardell - Staff Nurse

Mrs M Geeson - Senior Staff Nurse

Mrs M G Hunt - Occupational Health Nurse

Mrs K Lock - Bank Staff Nurse

Mrs P Measures - Night Sister

Mrs C Morris - Staff Nurse

Miss A J Poole - Staff Nurse

Mrs J Quincey - Occupational Health Nurse

Mrs M Reet - Staff Nurse

Mrs V Roper - Bank Staff Nurse

Miss J Sargeant - Student Nurse

Miss C Smith - Student Nurse

Mrs L Vowles - Enrolled Nurse

Mr D Wiles - Night Charge Nurse
Mrs C Winser - Bank Staff Nurse
Miss J Wood - Student Nurse

Nursing Auxiliaries

Mrs S Bett
Mrs L Davies
Mr A Greenslade
Mrs N Shelbourne
Miss W Sorrell

Physiotherapists

Ms B Myers - Senior Physiotherapist
Mrs J Starling - Junior Physiotherapist
Mrs S Thomas - Superintendent Physiotherapist

Laboratory Staff

Mr A Wills - Senior Medical Laboratory Scientific Officer

Staff of Queen's Medical Centre, Nottingham:

Dr D Fagan - Consultant Paediatric Pathologist
Professor Sir David Hull - Professor of Child Health
Dr D I Johnston - Consultant Paediatrician
Dr V Noble - Paediatric Senior Registrar
Dr P Small - Consultant Paediatric Radiologist
Dr S Smith - Paediatric Registrar
Dr T Stephenson - Consultant Paediatrician

South Lincolnshire Health Authority:

Mr C Pearce - Director of Nurse Education/District Nurse Adviser
Dr B W Platts - Occupational Health Physician
Mr M T Townson - District General Manager

<u>Trent Regional Health Authority:</u>

Professor R Alderslade - Regional Director of Public Health/
Regional Medical Officer
Mr B Edwards - Regional General Manager

<u>Other Witnesses:</u>

Mr B Blissett - District General Manager, Southern Derbyshire
Health Authority
Dr J Burn - Consultant Paediatrician, Bolton General Hospital
Dr J Carruthers - Chairman of the Association of NHS
Occupational Physicians
Mr P Chapman - Professional Officer, UNISON
Detective Superintendent S Clifton - Lincolnshire Constabulary
Ms C Hancock - General Secretary, Royal College of Nursing
Mr R Henley - Chief Medical Laboratory Scientific Officer
Supra-Regional Assay Service, University Hospital of Wales
Professor S R Meadow - Professor of Paediatrics and Child Health,
St James' University Hospital, Leeds
Dr M Patel - General Practitioner
Mr T J Pert - HM Coroner, Grantham District
Dr A Rimmer - Consultant Occupational Health Physician, Northern
General Hospital, Sheffield
Professor D Southall - Professor of Paediatrics, University of
Keele
Mr M Stonebridge-Foster - Coroner's Officer
Dr S Woodhead - Laboratory Director/ Reader in Endocrine
Chemistry, Supra-Regional Assay Service, University of Wales

<u>Parents:</u>

Mr and Mrs D A Crampton
Mr and Mrs A Davidson
Mr F Desmond
Mr and Mrs R Elstone
Mrs J Gibson

Mr and Mrs J King
Mrs C Peasgood
Mr and Mrs D Peck
Mr and Mrs C Taylor

SUBMISSIONS

Written submissions were received from several of those who appeared as witnesses before the Tribunal. Submissions were also received from the following organisations, which were not represented by a witness listed above.

Action for Sick Children
Association of British Paediatric Nurses (ABPN)
British Medical Association
British Paediatric Association
English National Board for Nursing, Midwifery and Health Visiting
Mid-Trent College of Nursing and Midwifery
The Society of Occupational Medicine

MEMBERSHIP AND SUMMARY OF OPERATION

1.   The Tribunal of Inquiry was chaired by Sir Cecil Clothier, KCB, QC, formerly Parliamentary Commissioner for Administration and Health Service Commissioner. The other members were Miss C Anne MacDonald, RGN, RSCN, DipN (London), Director of Quality, Manchester Children's Hospitals, incorporating the Royal Manchester Children's Hospital and Booth Hall Children's Hospital, and Professor David Shaw, CBE, FRCP, FRCP (Edin), Emeritus Professor of Clinical Neurology at the University of Newcastle upon Tyne.

2.   The Tribunal met on 35 occasions between Monday 7th June 1993 and Wednesday 26th January 1994. They interviewed 94 witnesses in person and received written answers to their questions from one further witness who was out of the country. All the parents of Allitt's victims were invited to give evidence to the Inquiry and one or both parents of nine of the children did so. The Tribunal also received ten written submissions from interested bodies, some of which also gave evidence in person through a representative. The Tribunal reviewed many thousands of pages of relevant documents.

3.   The Tribunal met twice in Grantham, first to visit Grantham and Kesteven General Hospital and secondly to meet with parents of Allitt's victims. The remainder of the meetings were held in London at the offices of Messrs Davies, Arnold, Cooper, Solicitors. The Tribunal was assisted by Ms Joanne Jackson and Ms Stephanie Panting.

MANAGEMENT STRUCTURE - WARD FOUR, FEBRUARY 1991

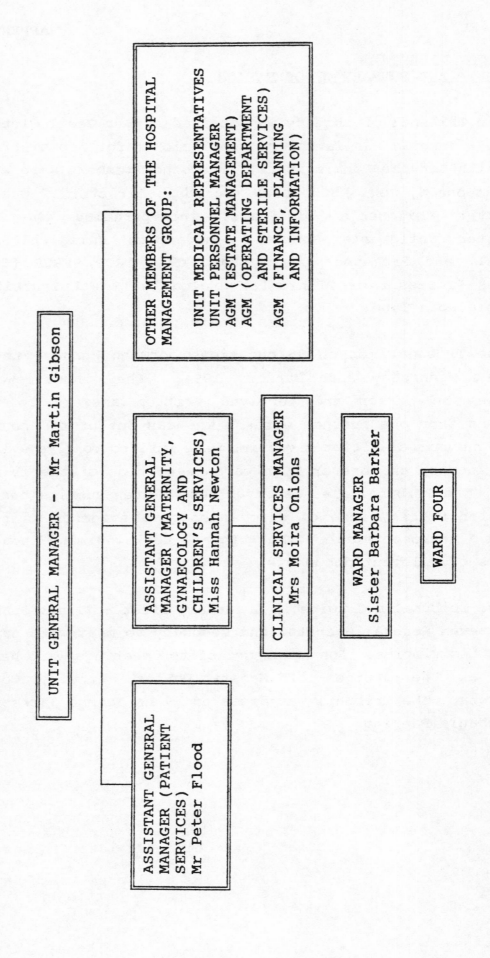

UNIT GENERAL MANAGER - Mr Martin Gibson

ASSISTANT GENERAL MANAGER (PATIENT SERVICES) Mr Peter Flood

ASSISTANT GENERAL MANAGER (MATERNITY, GYNAECOLOGY AND CHILDREN'S SERVICES) Miss Hannah Newton

OTHER MEMBERS OF THE HOSPITAL MANAGEMENT GROUP:

UNIT MEDICAL REPRESENTATIVES
UNIT PERSONNEL MANAGER
AGM (ESTATE MANAGEMENT)
AGM (OPERATING DEPARTMENT AND STERILE SERVICES)
AGM (FINANCE, PLANNING AND INFORMATION)

CLINICAL SERVICES MANAGER Mrs Moira Onions

WARD MANAGER Sister Barbara Barker

WARD FOUR

CHRONOLOGY OF EVENTS

February 1991

Tuesday 19th February	Beverly Allitt began work as an enrolled nurse on Ward Four.
Saturday 23rd February	Liam Taylor collapsed and died.

March 1991

Tuesday 5th March	Timothy Hardwick died suddenly.
Sunday 10th March	Kayley Desmond collapsed twice and was transferred to Queen's Medical Centre, Nottingham (QMC).
Saturday 23rd March	Paul Crampton suffered his first hypoglycaemic episode.
Sunday 24th March	Paul Crampton's second hypoglycaemic episode.
Thursday 28th March	Paul Crampton's third hypoglycaemic episode, following which he was transferred to QMC.
Saturday 30th March	Bradley Gibson collapsed and was transferred to QMC.
Sunday 31st March	Yik Hung Chan collapsed twice and was transferred to QMC.

April 1991

Thursday 4th April	Becky Phillips was discharged from Ward Four.
Friday 5th April	Becky Phillips collapsed at home in the early hours of the morning. She was dead on arrival at Grantham Hospital. Katie Phillips was admitted to Ward Four. She collapsed later in the day.
Sunday 7th April	Katie Phillips collapsed twice and was transferred to Nottingham City Hospital.

Tuesday 9th April	Michael Davidson collapsed.
Friday 12th April	Dr Nelson Porter was advised by telephone of the results of an insulin assay on a sample of Paul Crampton's blood taken during his third hypoglycaemic episode. The results showed that Paul's blood contained insulin which had been administered by injection.
Saturday 13th April	Christopher Peasgood collapsed twice and was transferred to QMC.
Sunday 14th April	Christopher King collapsed.
Tuesday 16th April	Christopher King collapsed three times and was transferred to QMC.
Thursday 18th April	Patrick Elstone collapsed twice and was transferred to QMC.
Monday 22nd April	Claire Peck collapsed twice and died following the second collapse.
Tuesday 30th April	Concerns about the events on Ward Four were reported to Grantham Police.

Printed in the United Kingdom for HMSO.
Dd.297646, C50, 2/94, 3396/4, 5673, 275451.